ENGLAND'S MUSICAL POET
THOMAS CAMPION

THERE IS A GARDEN

There is a Garden in her face, Where Roses and white Lillies grow;

A heauenly paradice is that place, wherein all pleasant fruits doe flow. There Cherries

grow which none may buy, Till Cherry ripe, till Cherry ripe, till Cherry ripe, Cherry ripe, ripe, ripe, Cherry

ripe, Cherry ripe themselues doe cry.

BASSVS.

2 Those Cherries fayrely doe enclose
Of Orient Pearle a double row,
Which when her lonely laughter showes,
They looke like Rose-buds fill'd with snow.
Yet them nor Peere, nor Prince can buy,
Till Cherry ripe themselues doe cry.

3 Her Eyes like Angels watch them still;
Her Browes like bended bowes doe stand,
Threatning with piercing frownes to kill
All that attempt with eye or hand
Those sacred Cherries to come nigh,
Till Cherry ripe themselues doe cry.

H 2

England's Musical Poet
THOMAS CAMPION

By
Miles Merwin Kastendieck

New York
RUSSELL & RUSSELL
1963

To My Father

PREFACE

THIS book serves to reveal, through a close scrutiny of the works of Thomas Campion, the interrelationship of poetry and music which created one of the great phenomena of English literature—the Elizabethan lyric. It presents an entirely new approach to Campion by recognizing in him the musician as poet and the poet-musician whereas in the past he has been considered only as a poet. He emerges the index and exponent of his age in its expression of poetry and music: England's Musical Poet.

In the course of treatment, I have shown how music had a material effect in conditioning the Elizabethan lyric, how poets wrote lyrics to be sung, and composers sought singable lyrics. Together they created an art form called the 'ayre' wherein poetry and music were equally balanced. In all probability many of the anonymous lyrics of the age originated in this manner, while Campion's 'ayres' attest the ability of one man to write both words and music. Since the secret of their effectiveness lies in associating words and notes together, the spontaneity of the Elizabethan lyric may be explained through the influence of music.

The book evolved from two circumstances: first, the comparatively recent monumental edition of the Elizabethan songbooks by Dr. Edmund H. Fellowes; and secondly, the juxtaposition of the study of English literature and the study of music in my pursuit of education culminating in graduate work at Yale. Without Percival Vivian's authoritative edition of Campion's Works and Dr. Fellowes' scholarly achievement, this book *could not have been written. Even with these, it was necessary to consult the originals, and I am grateful to the authorities of the Harvard Library for photostats of the 1601 Booke of Ayres, and of the British Museum for photostats of the other songbooks.*

I welcome this opportunity to thank a triumvirate of Yale professors for their help: John M. Berdan, for his thorough belief in my ideas; Alexander M. Witherspoon, for his critical appraisal of the manuscript; and Bruce Simonds, for his defence of the musical interpretation. To these should be added William Lyon Phelps, for his infectious enthusiasm upon reading the finished book; and Dorothea Walker Edge, for her meticulous proof-reading of the manuscript.

M.M.K.

February 1938

CONTENTS

ENGLAND'S MUSICAL POET
THOMAS CAMPION

I

WORDS AND MUSIC IN THREE
CENTURIES OF SONG

THE history of English verse from the beginning
of the seventeenth century to the present day is
largely the record of the separation of music and poetry.
The fact that the present status of the two arts is such
that they are usually considered to be self-sufficient
indicates that time has wrought many changes in the
close relationship that existed between them in Elizabethan England when one was recognized as the necessary complement of the other. For the more carefully we
study Elizabethan song and verse, the more inseparable
does this relationship appear.

Since 1600, music, chiefly under the influence of German inspiration, has evolved an art of its own in the man-
ifestation of such forms as the fugue, the suite, the so-
nata, and the symphony. But in England, it gradually
lost ground through the centuries so that until only recently has it again assumed a definite place in national
life. On the other hand, poetry, after being divested of its
musical setting and serving an apprenticeship in a period
of artificial poetical theory and practice in eighteenth-
century England, acquired an inherently poetical music
of its own in the Romantic Revival. It became customary
to speak of the music *in* poetry because of the newly
awakened interest and appreciation of the melodic possi-

bilities innate in the English language itself. English poets and composers had become so estranged by the nineteenth century that it was not only practically impossible but quite unnecessary to create musical settings for poems like 'Tintern Abbey,' 'Christabel,' 'St. Agnes' Eve,' 'Ode to the West Wind,' or 'To a Skylark.' Occasional exceptions might be noted in the works of Robert Burns and Thomas Moore, but generally poems were considered complete in themselves.

At the beginning of the nineteenth century, the art-song, that is to say, a song for solo voice with an elaborate instrumental accompaniment, became established on the continent through the genius of Schubert. He is acknowledged to be the one composer to instil a new spirit into the writing of songs. Since the general conception of song that prevails today dates from Schubert and is, therefore, little over a century and a quarter old, the art-song appears to be the natural outcome of the diverging lines which music and poetry were following in the nineteenth century.

Schubert bridged the gap between poet and composer through the artistic combination of his sensitiveness to the expressive qualities of poetry and his recognition of the expressive resources of music. Knitting the poetry in music to the music suggested in poetry, he evolved a type of song notable for its melodic refinement and its freedom of form. It was an individualized creation, subjective and emotional, and dependent on the delineation of detail for its effects. The song had become the expression of the composer's art. The poet supplied the words. The composer clothed the words in a musical setting based on his personal interpretation of the poet's conception. At first, these settings consisted of a melody for the voice and an accompaniment for the piano, both derived from the spirit of the words. Schubert's peerless gift for melody linked with his sense of the lyrical connotation of the words helped him to find ideal settings for such poems as 'Hark, Hark, the Lark' and 'Gretchen at the Spinning-wheel'—settings which make these songs representative of this new type. In the same style did Schumann, Franz, Brahms, and Wolf write their songs, each, however, asserting his individuality in the selection of details.

While the art-song developed on the continent, English song dropped to its lowest level. The attempts of a few nineteenth-century composers are practically unimportant historically. One notable exception, the songs of the Gilbert and Sullivan operas, has no place in an historical development but stands out as a luminous spot in a period of almost two centuries of darkness. They are typically English songs in form, content, and style, but representative not of the England of the nineteenth century so much as of the Elizabethan age.

The more firmly the art-song became an established musical form, the more did the accompaniment dominate both the voice and the melody. In this development, the music constantly asserted itself more and more, the poetry apparently receded into the background. Mendelssohn found that words were not so essential to a well-written melodic line. He consequently composed piano pieces which he called 'songs without words.' Liszt saw in the refinement of Schubert's melodies the possibilities of piano transcriptions in which the melody lost its iden-

tity with the words. A later development appeared in
which the piano accompaniment gave place to accompaniments written or arranged for quartets or quintets. The
Chanson Perpétuelle of Chausson, in its arrangement for
voice and quintet, is an effective example. Finally, a combination arose in which the voice merely recited the
words to an orchestral accompaniment as in the setting of
Alfred Noyes' poem, 'The Highwayman,' to the music
written for it by Deems Taylor. Thus the breach between
poet and composer grew steadily wider.

By the end of the nineteenth century, this evolution of
the art-song had given rise to several problems utterly unknown to Elizabethan song-writers. Two of them are rel-
evant to this discussion. The first of these is to what extent music begins where the words leave off; the second,
to what extent words may be sung arbitrarily to almost
any music.

As distinguished from the simplicity of Elizabethan
song in which we shall recognize the words and the music as complementary to each other—for poet and composer were working toward the same end—the chief characteristics of the art-song suggest that the composer has
put the meaning behind the poet's words, not usually designed for music, into an elaborate musical accompaniment. He appears to have attached the music to the
words. But the successful composer of art-songs, in creating the music for the words, has caught the mood and
thought of the poet, absorbed it, and reproduced it in
sound. If, in the act of creation, he may not have paid as
strict attention to the structure of the poem as he ought,
or perhaps upon publication failed to acknowledge the

poet's contribution, then the poet may quarrel with the composer over the result. But this difference of opinion between them as individuals does not indicate the incompatibility of the two arts of poetry and music. Has not the poet put the sense of rhythm, melody, and emotion behind music into words? Schubert's *Erlkönig* is a striking example in which the music is complementary to the words and the words complementary to the sound. The composer illustrates the actual words of Goethe's poem by characterizing the father, the son, and the frost king in the melodic modulations; by depicting the rider and his horse in the rhythmic accompaniment; by recording the terror of the child in the harsh dissonances between melody and bass notes; and by reaching the same dramatic climax as the poet did at the words: 'In his arms the boy lay dead.' The ideal interpretation of the relationship of music and poetry therefore appears to be

that poetry is a semicircle, and music begins at the diameter enclosing it and adds the complement of the circle; that there is no gap between poetry and music and nothing superfluous, that they fit exactly, even that one is incomplete without the other.

Few modern song-writers, except of course Schubert, have attained this goal as did the Elizabethans.

The observation that any music might fit the words, or that words might fit any melody, indicates that the whole understanding of the relationships of rhythm, melody, harmony, and emotional content in the fabric of song has not been grasped. These elements themselves determine the success of all songs since, to capture the atmosphere of a poem, a song must adequately represent as well as reproduce melodically and harmonically the spirit of the words. For these reasons, translations of the words of songs are never entirely successful, because the words and music are so interrelated that a change of language may throw the music out of all proportion to the words. A notable instance of this was Opitz's translation into German of the libretto of the Italian opera, *Dafne*. So poorly did the German words fit the Italian music that Heinrich Schutz was called upon to write appropriate music for the German words, and thus accidentally created the first German opera.

Among the chief requirements in the composition of the modern art-song is finding a melodic equivalent that clearly expresses the plain sense of the words. Schubert gave the art-song melody—melody of which the rise and fall should correspond to the meaning that the words imply. The questioning tone of the music in the first lines of *Who is Silvia?* is a good example of this tonal equivalence. It is the result of the tonal emphasis on the words *who* and *what*. Furthermore, if a poem has more than one stanza, it is probable that a different melody will be written for each, as the sense dictates, because the form of the art-song is free. The same tune, however, may serve different words provided an appropriate combination of the sense of rhythm and words is effected. Schubert was less successful with the other verses of *Who is Silvia?* probably because he focused too much attention on a perfect setting for the first. His song would have been greater as a whole had it not been written in strophe form. In Elizabethan song, on the contrary, we shall see that the stanzaic form was usually successful because the melodies were less refined and more adaptable.

Closely connected with the melodic equivalence of the word sense is the rhythmical representation or the musical prosody of the poem. In English poetry monosyllables predominate and words exist rhythmically in more or less irregular groups and phrases so that the regular rhythmical equivalent demanded in modern music is achieved with considerable difficulty. The Elizabethans experienced no problem because the rhythmical principles of music and verse were freer in that period. But the nineteenth-century composer, Sir Arthur Sullivan, for example, because of the more restricted rhythm of modern music, found it necessary to study not a single line of verse but several lines at once in order to find a setting that was rhythmically correct for the whole. Arthur Lawrence in his book on *Sir Arthur Sullivan* lists eight sketches of various rhythmic schemes that Sullivan made for the following few lines of verse from Gilbert's libretto for *Yeomen of the Guard*:

> *Were I thy bride,*
> *Then all the World beside*
> *Were not too wide*
> * To hold my wealth of love,*
> *Were I thy bride.*

The rhythm finally chosen for them is distinguished by the careful handling of the unimportant or unaccented syllables, the symmetrical agreement of the musical rhythm with the natural grouping of the words when spoken, and the subtle charm attained through the balance between the phrase, 'Were I thy bride,' and its repetition.

Were   I thy   bride, Then   all   the world   beside Were   not   too   wide   To   hold   my
wealth   of   love, Were   I   thy   bride.

The final requirement of good song writing according to modern theory is the realization of the spirit of the poem by harmonically revealing its hidden meanings, its dramatic values, and its emotional content. This is to be attained through the general impression created by the tonal values and through the attention paid to details of phrasing. In *Gretchen at the Spinning Wheel*, Schubert achieved perfection by closely observing these principles. The spinning-wheel accompaniment delineates a picture only suggested by the poet. In creating this general impression, the composer heightens the emotional effect already attained by the simple, direct, pictorial treatment of the words. At the point where Gretchen remembers her lover's kiss, the spinning-wheel accompaniment gives way to a succession of chords as the result of a change of mood in the words. Schubert implies that at this point, Gretchen forgot to spin. In such delicately refined details art-song abounds and thus demands expert and sensitive treatment of the relationship of words and music. When the accompaniment overshadows the melody or the words seem secondary in importance when the song is sung, the cause may be the singer's interpretation or the composer's elaboration of a musical setting which has already conformed to the essential requirements outlined. In contrast to the spontaneity of Elizabethan song, the art-song relies on the artistic refinement of details for its effect.

But a consideration of the art-song is only a small part of the history of song itself, in fact, little more than the development of a century in a story that is centuries old. According to an historical point of view, the older type of song is essentially a lyric so entwined with music that words and notes are spontaneously created. It is generally distinguished from the art-song in that it seems to sing itself because of a certain naturalness and apparently artless expression of human emotion, while the art-song, because it is the product of an impulse of refinement and superimposed artistic qualities, must be studied to be sung. In the art-song, the music is suggested to a composer through his individual insight and study of the meaning of the words of a poem, but in this older type of song, the music is suggested by the sound of the poetry itself and is an intrinsic part of it. This older type, which was in existence in England during the late sixteenth and the early seventeenth centuries—long before the time of Schubert and his art-song—is therefore quite different from the general conception of song at large today. It flourished at a time when music was predominantly vocal

and poets were not only keenly aware of the musical inflections of poetry, but were also familiar with the melodies of folk-song. Poet and composer met on common
ground and considered poetry as music in words, music as
poetry in sound.

The separation of music and verse, which was mentioned at the beginning of the chapter, had been so thoroughly effected by the end of the seventeenth century
that eighteenth-century England, to all intents and
purposes, was entirely unaware of the existence of
Elizabethan song and the essential relationship between
poet and composer in Elizabethan days. The two arts
appeared in the eighteenth century to be partially united,
nevertheless, in the opera and oratorio which had been
imported into England from the continent. Ignorant of
what we know today about Elizabethan song, and aware
of the relationship in the prevailing musical forms, some
of the more esthetically-minded writers in the latter half
of the century experienced a desire for a closer union of
music and poetry and entered into earnest discussions of
its possibilities. All of these recognized, as Dr. Burney
points out, that

music and poetry, during the infancy of their cultivation, in
every country, are so closely connected, that it is impossible
to speak of one without the other; yet in proportion as those
arts advance toward perfection, they will not only become
more and more independent but have a legislation and a
language of their own.

That music and poetry *were* still in the infancy of the
possibilities of their cultivation at this period appears to
have been the general attitude. It found expression in the

opinions of the eminent musical historians Sir John Hawkins and Dr. Charles Burney, who said that

the art of singing had never been cultivated in England with
a view to the improvement of the voice, or the calling forth
those powers of expression and execution, of which we at
this time know it is capable; and as to solo-compositions for
instruments, the introduction of such among us was at a
period not much beyond the reach of the memory of persons
yet living . . . In short, the people of this country, about
the middle of the seventeenth century, began to entertain an
idea of what in music is termed fine air, and seemed in earnest
determined to cultivate it.

It was under such circumstances that Bayly, along with
his contemporaries, advanced his views of the possibilities of a closer relationship of the two arts. He stated
that

musick is the basis on which poetry and oratory can be ad-
vantageously erected, and by it can be truly judged of . . .
Musick, indeed, if traced up to its origin, will be found the
first and immediate daughter of nature, while poetry and
oratory are only near relations of musick . . . The musician and poet by the art of sounds, numbers, and elegance
of words, meet in concert, when they present to our senses
beautiful imitations of external objects, their figure and motion, etc.

Not only was the golden age of English music and
Elizabethan song unknown to the public generally but
even to special students of the Elizabethan period. One
writer, James Beattie, interested as he was in Spenserian
poetry, sensed the Elizabethan situation. Unconscious,
however, of the period when England was not only the

most poetical but probably the most musical of nations, he observed that music

never appears to the best advantage but with poetry for its interpreter: and I am satisfied, that though musical genius may subsist without poetical taste, and poetical genius without musical taste; yet these two talents united might accomplish nobler effects, than either could do singly . . . And if it be true, that all poetry is originally song, the most poetical nation would seem to have the fairest chance to become the most musical.

But not knowing Elizabethan song, eighteenth-century England turned to the music of Purcell and Händel, ironically enough according to modern views, as representative of the greatest period of English musical history. Now the difference between the work of these musicians and that of the Elizabethans lies not so much in the style of writing as in the nature of the result and how that result was obtained. Purcell and Händel matched the rise and fall of their notes to the rise and fall of the words so that the general effect was similar to that originally attained by the Elizabethans a century earlier. The characteristics of this Elizabethan style is the subject of later chapters. Like Bach in Germany, however, Händel and to a lesser extent Purcell gained their knowledge more from the Italians who used the same style in laying the foundations of opera in the early seventeenth century, than from the Elizabethans. As the French scholar Pirro, writing on the esthetic practice of Bach, observed:

dans sa musique chantée, Bach s'inspire du sens des paroles sur lesquelles il compose, pour former les motifs qui'il y joint. Il les modèle avec soin d'après les mots du texte, en s'efforçant d'interpreter, à l'aide d'images musicales, quelque chose des idées qui s'y trouvent exprimées. On reconnâit partout qui'il s'ingenie à les évoquer et qu'il tente de les représenter, aussi nettement et aussi complètement que possible. En cela, il suit la coutume des musiciens du XVIIᵉ siècle.

But Purcell, Händel, and Bach, in writing operas, oratorios, and cantatas, erected musical structures on words not essentially poetic and certainly not lyrical in the Elizabethan sense. Thus their work illustrates the beginning of the separation of music and poetry. By this time, furthermore, poet and composer had become individuals working independently of each other; the estrangement between them was steadily growing. On the other hand, the Elizabethan song-writers created true lyrical songs spontaneously. These were poetically and musically fused into one creation so that the inflection of the words suggested the music and the music underlined the words. Even when in later centuries the lyric was separated from the musical setting, the musical quality inherent in the lyric still continued to make itself felt to some extent. Poet and composer were either one and the same individual or were attuned to one another through the common knowledge of the music of poetry and the poetry of music from both a technical and artistic point of view.

Thus while art was becoming self-conscious during the eighteenth century and acquiring a formality that the Elizabethans never knew, music was undergoing a change from the polyphony of voices, which reached its highest expression in England at the end of the sixteenth century, to strict counterpoint for instruments. The complexities of vocal music were being ironed out in the rigid unity of instrumental fugues, the conventional dance patterns of delicate clavichord suites, or the strict form of the early sonatas and symphonies, while Elizabethan song, which had flowed smoothly and gracefully, was completely lost. After Purcell, English song underwent an eclipse. In its place came the ordered recitative of the oratorio and the conventional, vocalized arias of imported Italian opera. Poetry had become imprisoned in or chained to the heroic couplet. It was no longer sung or spoken with the inflections and intonations of natural speech but declaimed as so much oratory; the musical qualities had been replaced by the literary aspects of poetry. Poet and composer were definitely estranged, and as the gap grew wider each art evolved a legislation and language of its own.

II

MUSIC AND POETRY IN THE
ELIZABETHAN AGE

PROBABLY never before nor since those thirty years that mark the closing of the sixteenth and the opening of the seventeenth centuries has England been so *alive* to poetry, drama, and music. The reign of Queen Elizabeth has long been recognized as the golden age of English literature. Only within the last quarter century, however, has the realization come that this period also witnessed the culmination of the golden age of English music. Along with the favourable reception accorded the revival of their music has come the growing consciousness of the vital part that music played in the lives of the Elizabethans. The more firmly the realization is established, the more necessary it becomes to learn to what extent the predominance of music in the Elizabethan period could influence the literature.

Until very recently it was not customary to consider England the home of a musical people. But during the sixteenth century, music was so much in the air that everyone was influenced by it in some way or other. Davey reminds us that

it may justly be claimed that England was beyond question the most musical of nations during the flower-time of Gothic art . . . Of the music composed between 1550 and 1630 it is only the English which has secured a permanent hold.

Erasmus in his *Praise of Folly* tells us that

as Nature in her Dispensations of Conceitedness has dealt with *Private Persons*, so has she given a particular Smatch of Self-love to each *Country* and *Nation*. Upon this Account it is that the English challenge the Prerogative of having the most handsome Women, of being [the] most accomplished in the Skill of Musick, and of keeping the best Tables.

The history of English music reveals the love of the people for folk-song and country-dancing. Improvisation on an extensive scale in both of these natural forms of expression gave birth to a spontaneity and sincerity of unrestrained and unpremeditated music. Its origins are traceable through the days of the wandering minstrels to the carol and ballad eras which in themselves are a tribute to English music and folk-poetry. From the thirteenth century comes that well-constructed work, 'Sumer is icumen in,' which indicates a mastery of music hitherto unknown and for two centuries unchallenged. An Englishman named John Dunstable, who flourished about the middle of the fifteenth century, is often credited with supplying the impetus to a realization of the art of musical composition by his work in vocal polyphony. His school, however, was quickly superseded by that of the Netherland composers on the continent. From the reign of Henry VIII through that of Elizabeth and, carried on by its own momentum, into the reign of James I, music became the elixir of English life. In sacred music, England could boast of such great musicians as Tye, Whyte, Taverner, Tallis, and finally William Byrd. Henry Peachum, who is perhaps better known for his advice on the proper conduct for an Elizabethan gentleman than for his pertinent observations on music, speaks highly of Byrd. He says that

for Motets and Musicke of pietie and deuotion, as well for the honour of our Nation, as the merit of the man, I preferre aboue all other our *Phoenix*, M. *William Byrd*, whom in that kind, I know not whether any man equall. I am sure, none excell, euen by the iudgement of *France* and *Italy*, who are very sparing in the commendation of strangers, in regard of that conceipt they hold of themselues. His *Cantiones Sacrae*, as also his *Gradualia*, are meere Angelicall and Diuine; and being of himselfe naturally disposed to Grauitie and Pietie, his veine is not so much for light Madrigals or Canzonets, yet his *Virginella*, and some others in his first set, cannot be mended by the best *Italian* of them all.

After 1588 and before 1630, some two thousand madrigals, to say nothing of other forms of secular music, were printed. Books about the praise and the abuse of music and frequent editions of books on the playing of lutes and other instruments appeared. The popularity of psalm-singing was so general that numerous editions of the psalms with musical settings were published between 1560 and 1600. Burney tells us that

in the reign of Queen Mary all the Protestants, except those who courted martyrdom, sung these Psalms *sotto voce*; but after the accession of Queen Elizabeth, like orgies, they were roared aloud in almost every street, as well as church, throughout the kingdom.

With the Elizabethans, music was a passion. When Stephen Gosson, whose attack on poetry is so familiar but whose connection with music is less often considered, gave vent to a pleasant invective against the prevalence of music, he probably pictured the conditions most adequately.

Homer with his Musicke cured the sick Souldiers in the *Grecians* campe, and purged euery mans Tent of the Plague [he points out. But] thinke you that those miracles could bee wrought [now] with playing of Daunces, Dumpes, Pauins, Galiardes, Measures, Fancyes, or new streynes? They neuer came wher this grewe, nor knew what it ment . . . Were the *Argiues* and *Pythagoras* nowe aliue, and saw how many frets, how many stringes, how many stops, how many keyes, how many cliffes, how many moodes, how many flats, how many sharps, how many rules, how many spaces, how many noates, how many restes, how many querks, how many corners, what chopping, what changing, what tossing, what turning, what wresting and wringing is among our Musitions, I beleue verily, that they would cry out with the countryman: *Heu quod tam pingui macer est mihi taurus in aruo.*

Gosson may have been able to suggest the extensive interest in music, but he did not record the violent enthusiasm that existed. Music was found not only in song and dance alone. A contemporary, John Case, writes as follows:

What shall I speak of that pettie and counterfeit music which carters make with their whips, hempknockers with their beetles, spinners with their wheels, barbers with their sizzers, smithes with their hammers? where methinkes the master-smith with his treble hammer sings deskant whilest the greater buz upon the plainsong: Who doth not straitwaies imagin upon musick when he hears his maids either at the wool-hurdle or the milking pail? good God, what distinct intention and remission is there of their strokes? what orderly dividing of their straines? what artificial [artistic] pitching of their stops?

Such extravagance need not be taken too seriously, but combined with Gosson's comments it discloses a widespread interest among Elizabethans for expressing themselves musically.

The *locus classicus* for the musical spirit of the age is given by Chappell:

Tinkers sang catches; milkmaids sang ballads; carters whistled; each trade, and even the beggars, had their special songs; the base-viol hung in the drawing room for the amusement of waiting visitors; and the lute, cittern, and virginals, for the amusement of waiting customers, were the necessary furniture of the barber's shop. They had music at dinner; music at supper; music at weddings; music at funerals; music at night; music at dawn; music at work; music at play.

But if this is a picture of music at large in England, what was the extent of its cultivation in the home? Chappell says 'that no subject during this period, perhaps not even excepting religion, so much occupied men's minds.' There were, of course, no public concerts nor recitals, no orchestras nor chamber music ensembles. But music in the home was almost a daily occurrence. Nicholas Yonge, who introduced the Italian madrigal into England in 1588, makes the following interesting comment:

Since I first began to keepe house in this citie, it hath been no small comfort unto me, that a great number of gentlemen and merchants of good accompt . . . have taken in good part such entertainment of pleasure as my poore abilitie was able to affoord them, both by the exercise of Musicke daily used in my house, and by furnishing them with bookes of that kinde yeerely sent me out of Italy and other places.

Thomas Morley's famous story gives further evidence of this phase of musical cultivation.

And yesternight there were a number of excellent schollers, (both gentlemen and others:) but all the propose, which then was discoursed vpon, was Musicke . . . I was compelled to discouer mine owne ignorance, and confesse that I knew nothing at all in it . . . Among the rest of the guestes, by chaunce, master *Aphron* came thether also, who falling to discourse of Musicke, was in an argument so quickly taken vp & hotly pursued by *Eudoxus* and *Calergus*, two kinsmen of *Sophobulus*, as in his owne art he was ouerthrowne: but he still sticking in his opinion, the two gentlemen requested mee to examine his reasons, and confute them. But I refusing, & pretending ignorance, the whole companie condemned me of discurtesie, being fully perswaded, that I had beene as skilfull in that arte, as they tooke mee to be learned in others. But supper being ended, & Musicke bookes (according to the custome) being brought to the table: the mistresse of the house presented me with a part, earnestly requesting mee to sing; but when, after manie excuses, I protested vnfainedly that I could not, euerie one began to wonder. Yea, some whispered to others, demaunding how I was brought vp.

This story calls attention not only to the embarrassment of the young man on finding himself so wanting in the art of music, but also to his inability to sing. His predicament might be taken with a grain of salt were it not corroborated by Henry Peacham, who considered that music was a necessary requisite for the making of a complete gentleman. He says: 'I desire no more in you then to sing your part sure, and at first sight, withall, to plan the same vpon your Violl, or the exercise of the Lute, priuately to your selfe.' His reason for this was that 'I dare affirme, there is no one Science in the world, that so af-

fecteth the free and generous spirit, with a more delightful and in-offensiue recreation; or better disposeth the
minde to what is commendable and vertuous.'

There is no doubt that music was considered an essential part of education in England during this period. Degrees in music which had been conferred by Oxford and
Cambridge for over a century, were won by enterprising
men. In 1596, Elizabeth appointed John Bull, a recognized musician of the time, the first professor of music in
Gresham College. Furthermore, since music was highly
esteemed in the universities, the supposition is that it was
widely taught in the schools as well as fostered in the
home through private tutors. One of the best instances of
musical education at home is the episode of Bianca's lute
lessons in *The Taming of the Shrew*.

Queen Elizabeth, an accomplished player on the virginals herself, delighted in being regaled during dinner 'with
twelve trumpets, and two kettledrums; which, together
with fifes, cornets, and side-drums, made the hall ring for
half an hour together.' The household musicians included at one time seventeen trumpeters, two lutenists,
two harpers, eight singers, six children singers, one re-
beck, nine minstrels, six sackbuts, eight viols, three
drumsleds, two flute players, two virginal players, eight
interlude players, and several foreigners.

Finally, music held an important place in the Eliza-
bethan play and playhouse. It was a musician, Richard
Farrant, who founded the Blackfriars Theatre in 1578.
And, as Cowling points out,

there is a chain of evidence ranging from *Gorboduc* in 1562 and
Gammer Gurton's Needle in 1566 to Prynne's *Histriomastix* in

1633 showing that music was a regular and important ingredient in the drama of Shakespeare's age . . . A song was almost a *sine qua non*, and was far more regular in its presence [in a dramatic show] than a fool or a clown. There is evidence to show that jigs and dances were performed during the interval between the acts [actions?].

Patrons of the drama demanded music, and performances usually ended with a variety of dances.

Music had been associated with the drama from the beginning of its evolution in the mystery plays. Into these plays crept secular songs which were common among the people. They became part of the lyric tradition which culminated in the seventeenth century. John Heywood, a musician in the court of Henry VIII, is usually considered the originator of the Tudor Interlude in which music played a considerable part. Finally, with the appearance of *Ralph Roister Doister* and *Gammer Gurton's Needle* the inclusion of comic songs and incidental music became fixed. They took their place in the Elizabethan play because of tradition and the demand for music. The dramatists in their practical way were not slow in realizing the effects obtainable in the use of music. Play after play reveals the growing fusion of the songs with the text, and the significant use of stage directions for musical effects. So widespread a popularity made music indispensable to Elizabethan drama. Furthermore, the dramatists in this age were poets, not playwrights. With an incentive to write songs for plays, they produced some of the finest in the language.

The songs in Shakespeare's plays attest the demand for them. But since contemporary music for most of them is unknown, little attention has been paid to the method of their creation. Richmond Noble believes 'that Shakespeare wrote the songs with some melody in view, and a close scrutiny of the stops used in the songs strengthens that view, for many of them are obviously inserted to meet a singer's requirements, to enable him at suitable intervals to rest his voice.' Shakespeare's knowledge of popular songs and ballads was certainly extensive. The Gravedigger's song in *Hamlet*, the 'Willow Song' in *Othello*, and finally the snatches of Ophelia's mad songs all come from popular sources. Noble further points out that 'every one of Shakespeare's songs seems to have been written or adapted expressly for the play in which it appears and for the character to whom it is assigned.' But into the details of this subject we cannot enter.

There remains for brief comment the astonishing number of musical allusions to be found in Shakespeare's plays. His frequent puns, for instance, in the *Taming of the Shrew*, *Hamlet*, and numerous other plays, could hardly have been made had he not been thoroughly familiar with the technical terms of vocal and lute music. All this is part of the musical parlance so common to the poetry of the period. Though references to music could become a literary convention as easily as anything else, still there was more behind them than mere fashionable usage. Indirectly, they again testify to the domination of music. The famous passage in Act V of *The Merchant of Venice*,

> *The man that hath no music in himself,*
> *Nor is not mov'd with concord of sweet sounds,*
> *Is fit for treasons, stratagems and spoils.*

might be dismissed as an extemporization on the theme of music according to Elizabethan convention. But when Henry Peacham writes in a similar vein with far different motives the case is altered. Peacham says:

I know there are many . . . of such disproportioned spirits, that they auoide her companie . . . I dare not passe so rash a censure of these as *Pindar* doth, or the *Italian*, hauing fitted a prouerbe to the same effect, *Whom God loues not, that man loues not Musicke*; but I am verily perswaded, they are by nature very ill disposed, and of such a brutish stupiditie, that scarce any thing else that is good and sauoureth of vertue, is to be found in them.

The many musical references in Shakespeare indicate his great absorption in music just as his songs disclose the influence exerted by music.

Ben Jonson was also influenced. He used music to introduce characters and promote the plot because he recognized the musical enthusiasm of the age as well as the dramatic advantages in the use of songs. A close study of his plays proves this. Furthermore, when Jonson found it necessary to prepare a lyric for music, he did so with charm and easy grace. As W.M.Evans says:

The nearer his lyrics approach song-form, the more flowing, the more singable, the more readable the poetry. The greater the stress under which he labored to satisfy the musicians, the more tuneful the lyric. Music taught Jonson to write light, melodious verse, and to arrange the pattern of a masque . . . And we find that the stanzas which were made for song are the same poems editors and collectors seek out for their anthologies. They are the stanzas critics praise most highly for their lyrical excellence.

That the union of music and poetry in the Elizabethan period existed as a natural phenomenon cannot be over-emphasized. The significant fact about such a relation-ship was that the music was predominantly vocal. With the rise of instrumental composition when music became independent of song and developed an art of its own, the possibilities of a reunion became more and more remote. As the musical element became less and less apparent in seventeenth-century poetry, the purely literary aspects became more prominent. But in the Elizabethan age, po-etry like music was vocal. On this plane, therefore, the two arts were united.

Richard Barnfield's sonnet still stands as a perfect trib-ute to this union of music and poetry. He wrote that

> *If music and sweet poetry agree,*
> *As they needs must (the sister and the brother),*
> *Then must the love be great twixt thee and me,*
> *Because thou lov'st the one, and I the other.*
> *Dowland to thee is dear; whose heavenly touch*
> *Upon the lute doth ravish human sense:*
> *Spenser to me; whose deep conceit is such,*
> *As passing all conceit, needs no defence.*
> *Thou lov'st to hear the sweet melodious sound*
> *That Phoebus' lute (the Queen of Music) makes:*
> *And I in deep delight am chiefly drowned*
> *When as himself to singing he betakes.*
>   *One God is God of both (as poets feign),*
>   *One knight loves both, and both in thee remain.*

The miscellanies and the song books are the eternal evi-dence of this relationship. When the words of Elizabethan songs were not written by the composers of the music, they were written with the distinct purpose in some poet's mind of having them set to music. From the *Paradyse of daynty deuices* of 1576 in which appears probably the first lyric 'In commendation of Musick'—written by the poet-dramatist-musician Richard Edwards—to the *Phoenix Nest* of 1593, the style of the lyrics is indicative of this purpose. Any doubt of this is obliterated after looking at the dedications of these miscellanies. For instance, the dedication of the *Paradyse of daynty deuises* states that the book was printed because 'the ditties [were] both pithy and pleasant, as well for the inuention as meter, and wyll yeelde a farre greater delight, being as they are so aptly made to be set to any song in 5 partes, or song to instrument.'

The curious treatment that these songs have received during the centuries is illustrated by the miscellany *A Handefull of pleasant delites*. The printer told his readers that:

> *You that in Musicke do delight*
> *your minds for to solace:*
> *This little book of sonets (might)*
> *wel like you in that case. etc.*

He called them sonnets. Today, the title, sonnet, means a poem of fourteen lines written according to a certain prescribed style. In the Elizabethan age, a sonnet was practically a synonym for a song. The titles of various collections of lyrics from Tottel's *Songs and Sonnets* in 1557 to the *Songs and Sonnets* in John Donne's collected works of 1633, make this interpretation acceptable. In the case of this particular miscellany, the sonnets are now recognized as broadside ballads written for definite tunes current at the time and tunes that would be familiar to any contemporary reader of the book. This fact gives us the first glimpse into the relationship of music and poetry in the Elizabethan age. Naturally in writing a poem to the tune of, let us say *Greensleeves*, which was a common dance tune, the writer was necessarily forced to fit his words to the music to some degree. His meter was therefore already provided. The rhythm of these ballads must go back to the rhythms of dances. To establish this fact further, note that Webbe, who in common with other contemporary critics of poetry often makes references to music, says in the course of his *Discourse on English Poetry*:

neither is there anie tune or stroke which may be sung or plaide on instruments which hath not some poetical ditties framed according to the numbers thereof, some to Rogero, some to Trenchmore, to downe right Squire, to Gaillardes, to Pauines, to Iygges, to Brawles, to all manner of tunes which euerie Fidler knows better then my selfe.

Now dance tunes though perhaps the most popular were not the only musical melodies of the day, but they were among the many rhythms and melodic forms which were available to poets who were writing with the express purpose of having their ditties set to music. Sidney in his *Apologie for Poesie* says significantly that the poet 'beginneth not with obscure definitions, which must blur the margent with interpretations, and load the memory with doubtfulnesse; but hee commeth to you with words sent [*sic*] in delightfull proportion, either accompanied with, or prepared for, the well inchaunting skill of Mu-

sicke.' Puttenham in his *Arte of English Poesie* introduces
us to the whole situation by speaking thus of

our poeticall proportion, which holdeth of the Musical: Poesie
is a skill to speake & write harmonically: and verses or rime
to be a kind of Musicall vtterance, by reason of a certain
congruitie in sounds pleasing the eare, though not perchance
so exquisitely as the harmonicall concents of the artificial
Musicke, consisting in strained notes, as is the vocall Musicke;
or that of melodious instruments, as Lutes, Harpes, Regals,
Records, and such like.

This general relationship of music and verse in Elizabethan song is akin to that fostered by the French Pleiade
during the same century. Ronsard was the brightest star
in this constellation. His theories that poetry when not
allied to music was lacking in a certain completeness, and
that music without the melody of poetry was lifeless, are
identical with those in practice in Elizabethan England.
The common source of such theories is the prevalence of
vocal music. The influence of the Pleiade in England unquestionably contributed to the Elizabethan lyric. But
however French the form might appear to be, the result
was typically English. The tradition of English music
and poetry was too deeply rooted to have its course
changed to any marked degree. The union was common
to both countries. French influence may have added a certain richness to Elizabethan song, but its substance was
English.

Thus music inspired the writing of many Elizabethan
lyrics which are now valued for their literary charm.
Would these lyrics, which so enrich the literature of the
golden age, have existed if the popular demand for music

had not been so pronounced and music such an intrinsic part of Elizabethan life? They were born in an era of practical song when music and poetry were on an equal footing and united in such a way that when both elements are known either one appears incomplete without the other.

III

THE CASE FOR THOMAS CAMPION

IN the heart of this world of music and poetry lived Thomas Campion,—poet, musician, and 'Doctor in Physicke.' Well known and held in the highest esteem as a writer of exquisite ayres in his day, he was soon forgotten after his death. One song, *What if a day*, was still popular in 1663; but the majority of his ayres passed quickly into oblivion with the rest of the Elizabethan song-books. From 1620 to 1887 Campion was lost to the world. In general, the eighteenth century never knew him. Sir John Hawkins found room for a page summary of the few stray facts that he could gather about Campion as a musician, but that is the only acknowledgement of him made during that period. The nineteenth century paid little attention to him. He was not to be found among the poets in Palgrave's *Golden Treasury* of 1861, and the references to him which were made by Brydges (1814), Haslewood (1815), and Arber (1877), passed practically unnoticed.

Not until the closing decades of the century was interest in Campion aroused. The year 1887 saw his revival in the publication of A.H.Bullen's *Lyrics from the Elizabethan Song-books*, and 1889, the *editio princeps* of his works. Bullen's enthusiasm over the fact that 'there are no songs in our language more graceful, happy, and unconstrained—with more melody and magic—than many that

we find in Campion's song-books,' caught the attention
of both critics and the public, and Campion was at once
hailed as a writer endowed with the true lyric impulse.
The literary critics greeted his renaissance with enthusi-
astic eulogies over the freshness and spontaneity of his
lyrics long since shorn of their musical settings. Campion
became established as a distinguished Elizabethan lyric
poet.

So fervent was the reception of this revival that Bullen
prefixed to the second edition in the *Muses Library* in
1903, the following warning:

In 1887 Campion's admirers were few indeed. By critics and
anthologists he had been persistently neglected. I·pleaded that
the time had come for him to take his rightful place among
our English poets; and the plea was so successful that he now
runs the risk of becoming the object of uncritical adulation.

In 1909, Percival Vivian published the scholarly edition
of Campion's works. Reviewing this book for the *Nation*,
Stuart Sherman observed that 'it argues something immortal in Campion that he has survived his revival. We
have not now to record the beginning, but the establishment, of his second reputation, which bids fair to prove
more durable than the first.' Nine selections from Campion now grace the pages of the *Oxford Book of English
Verse*. But even today, Campion's unique position is not
fully recognized.

When his works were brought to light, the critics in
their enthusiasm did not entirely forget to attribute the
freshness and spontaneity of the lyrics to the marriage of
the words to the music which they recognized as a characteristic of the Elizabethan age. Still, they did not hesi-

tate to grant a divorce to this union. The general misconception of Elizabethan music was still prevalent. The
critics were not very musical; they felt no need for the
music; they were even offended at the suggestion that the
words might be incomplete without the musical settings.
Bullen himself is described by W.B.Yeats as a 'fine
scholar in poetry who hates all music but that of poetry,
and knows of no instrument that does not fill him with
rage and misery.' Consequently, Campion's new reputation was built to a large degree on his merits as a poet.
The fact that he was in reality *a musical poet* guided by
music to lyrical heights, was quite naturally not comprehended.

This curious misconception of Campion's true status is
not as strange as it may appear. It was, in fact, a traditional oversight on the part of critics, literary scholars,
and even professors of poetry to ignore the musical settings of Elizabethan lyrics. The tendency to separate the
poetry from the music in published collections of the
words of Elizabethan songs might be first observed as far
back as the appearance of *Tottel's Miscellany* in 1557. But
in the case of this and the other Elizabethan miscellanies,
mentioned in the preceding chapter, the music for the
words of these lyrics was undoubtedly familiar in those
times. Separation of the words from the music did not
mean failure to associate the two. The situation was similar to that of the modern hymnal in which only the
words are printed yet the music is well known. Probably
most if not all Elizabethan lyrics were closely associated
with music. Either the authors had written them for musical settings, or they themselves had written both the

words and the music. But like the songs, sonnets, and ballads in the miscellanies, these lyrics have been printed without the music. Because of the loss of much of the music and because of the anonymity of so many of the lyrics, the significance of the influence of the music on the poetry has been overlooked. The publication of Percy's *Reliques* in 1765 devoid of any suggestion of the connection of these ballads with music, is another striking instance of how the old musical tradition had been forgotten.

When, therefore, the Elizabethan song-books were discovered, the relationship between music and poetry might have been suggested had the song-books been printed intact with words and music. But the general dearth of knowledge of the style of Elizabethan music until only recently, lessened this possibility. Consequently, the words were gathered from their musical setting and published separately as lyrics, while the music was left behind in the song-books. The charm of the lyrics themselves and the newly awakened interest in Elizabethan music, however, have so brought the two together that the old relationship between them is now discernible.

The wedlock of music and poetry, which, as we have seen, was characteristic of the Elizabethan age, finds its best exponent in Thomas Campion. His unique position can be comprehended only when both his poetry and his music are considered side by side as single creations. He was the natural product of the environment in which he lived. Undoubtedly, he was one of many musical poets who lived at the time, but who so far continue to remain anonymous. Whether his contemporaries are known or unknown, however, Campion probably represents the finest expression of the union of the two arts in this period. In an age of dramatists, of course, Campion is hardly more than a minor figure; but in an age of poetry, he assumes a more important position because he often rose to the lyric heights of Shakespeare and had traits common with the early Milton. Camden placed him among some of the most famous men of his time in 1605. This is his citation:

These may suffice for some Poeticall descriptions of our auncient Poets, if I would come to our time, what a world could I present to you out of Sir Philipp Sidney, Ed. Spencer, Samuel Daniel, Hugh Holland, Ben: Iohnson, Th. Campion, Mich. Drayton, George Chapman, Iohn Marston, William Shakespeare, & other most pregnant witts of these our times, whom succeeding ages may iustly admire.

In an age of song, however, Campion as both a poet and a composer stands first among the song-writers. Any re-estimation of Elizabethan poetry must give him a larger place than he has been assigned hitherto because he is the index of his age in its expression of the union of music and poetry.

Campion, then, is to be considered *more* than a poet. He was both a poet *and* a musician. He must, therefore, be introduced again as *a musical poet* in the true meaning of the words. The music that swayed so many poets was part of his creative work. He did not write poems, but 'ayres.' If, in writing these ayres, he excelled as a poet, that is all the more to his credit. To call him a lyric poet while recognizing only his literary achievement is to present half an artist. He must be considered a lyric poet in the oldest meaning of the word, that is to say, a musical poet.

Born in London on Ash Wednesday, the twelfth of February 1567, Thomas Campion was the second child of John and Lucy Campion.[1] His father, Cursitor of the Chancery Court, and a member of the Inner Temple, was considered a gentleman, not wealthy but comfortably situated. Both parents died during the boy's childhood, but before her death, Lucy Campion, *née* Searle, had married again. Campion's stepfather married shortly after his mother's death so that Campion found himself, at fourteen, an orphan with an unsympathetic stepfather and his new wife. Packed off to Peterhouse, Cambridge, with his half-brother, Thomas Sisley by name, 'he seems to have imbibed a considerable and varied knowledge of classical literature, together with much reverence for it.' His interest in medicine may have been aroused while in attendance, since Peterhouse, at this time in one of its most flourishing periods, fostered interest in both foreign travel and medicine. He left Cambridge, however, in April 1584, without taking a degree.

By 1586, Campion was enrolled at Gray's Inn where he probably derived more from the social contacts than from the study of law which, according to his Latin epigrams, failed to interest him. In the course of his residence, he took part in the plays, masques, and revels which were part of the social activities of the Inns of Court. He was

1. For these facts I have used Vivian's introduction, Chapter I, as the latest authority. Bullen contributed the main facts in 1889. Haslewood in 1815 covered only part of the ground. *Campion's Works*, Oxford, 1909, by Percival Vivian.

also writing Latin epigrams and English verse. As was the custom in those days, the manuscripts of these poems were circulated freely among his friends and associates. 'In 1591, his first printed poems, the set of five anonymous "Cantos" included in the *Poems and Sonets of Sundry other Noblemen and Gentlemen* appended to Newman's surreptitious edition of Sidney's *Astrophel and Stella*, appeared' while other poems were to be found in the common-place books. Vivian seems justified in believing that Campion accompanied the expedition of the Earl of Essex to Dieppe to assist Henri IV in 1591, 'as a Gentleman Adventurer, probably attached to Carey's London contingent.' But Campion was back at Gray's Inn before the termination of that expedition, and remained there until 1595 when his *Poemata*, a work of epigrams and youthful poems in Latin, was published.

Shortly after the appearance of the *Poemata*, Campion was 'regarded as the second English writer of Latin epigrams, Sir Thomas More having been the first . . . As a Latin elegist, however, Campion arrogates to himself the first place in Elegeia I of this 1595 collection.' These Latin poems reveal Campion as a young man with epicurean tastes sowing his wild oats 'with the thoroughness of an inflammable disposition.' The pleasant things of life were: faithful friends, fair women, music, and poetry; the unpleasant, lawyers, ugly women, and shallow persons.

By 1602, Campion was considered by Samuel Daniel to be 'a man of faire parts and good reputation.' Just when and where he qualified as a physician, is unknown. According to Vivian, this must have occurred at a foreign university between the years 1602 and 1606. Once a Doctor, however, Campion practised until his death, gaining a considerable reputation as a physician.

Campion's connection with Sir Thomas Monson, to whom he dedicated his *Third and Fourth Booke of Ayres*, involved him in the famous Overbury murder case. The implications against him were of slight account. Objections to the Earl of Somerset's marriage to the divorced Countess of Essex had caused an open break between the earl, then Viscount Rochester, and Sir Thomas Overbury. The outcome was Overbury's horrible death and the completion of the plans for the wedding on 26 December 1613. Campion wrote a beautiful masque for the occasion. In 1615, however, an inquiry into the murder brought about an examination of Campion and the arrest of Monson. Campion had acted as an agent for Monson but since 'he knew not for what consideration the money was paid,' it is unnecessary to give further details of the charge. Monson, who was not guilty of any part in the conspiracy, was pardoned in February 1617. Shortly after this, Campion's book appeared.

Apart, then, from his practice of medicine and the writing and publication of his various works, Campion's life appears to have been that of an agreeable and probably contented bachelor. He died on 1 March 1620, leaving 'All that he had . . . and wished that his estate had bin farr more' to his friend, Philip Rosseter.

Campion authorized the publication of some of his ayres in 1601. They appeared in *A Booke of Ayres, Set foorth to be song to the Lute, Orpherian, and Base Violl*, by Philip Rosseter, Lutenist. The significance of this work will be discussed in the next chapter. The following year his *Obseruations in the Art of English Poesie* was published. It immediately became the cause of many contemporary and later mistaken notions on Thomas Campion's apparent opposition to rime though he continued to write beautiful riming lyrics. In both these works Campion may be studied as the musician and poet. In 1607, he wrote the *Discription of A Maske . . . in honour of the Lord Hayes* disclosing his potentialities as a poet-musician. The year 1613 witnessed the appearance of two more masques, one known as the *Lords Maske*, the other as the so-called *Squires Maske* in honour of the Earl of Somerset; a masque-entertainment presented by Lord Knowles to amuse Queen Anne during her progress to Bath; the *Songs of Mourning* for Prince Henry, and probably about this time the *Two Bookes of Ayres*, of which the first contained 'Diuine and Morall Songs,' the second, 'Light Conceits of Louers.' By 1617 the *Third and Fourth Bookes of Ayres* had appeared, and possibly about the same time, his other prose work, *A New Way of Making Fowre parts in Counter-point*. Another book of Latin epigrams in 1619 which included much of the contents of the 1595 edition, seems to have completed his list of works.

By the very nature of the titles of these publications it may be seen how peculiarly significant was Campion's position. He is a true child of the age during which music and poetry reached the zenith of their glory hand in hand. His ayres combine the two arts in the act of creation, and his prose treatises are of considerable importance in each of these respective arts. His masques are the natural outcome of the period and his own fitness to write in a form which was still unsettled.

But had it not been for Rosseter who knows whether Campion's ayres would have ever been printed? The anonymity of so many Elizabethan lyrics is probably the result of a certain non-professional attitude which prevailed in Elizabethan days among poets, pipers, and artists generally. The attitude was shared by Campion. Those lines in the dedication of *A Booke of Ayres* in 1601 are singularly important. Rosseter states that Campion's ayres were

made at his vacant houres, and priuately emparted to his friends, whereby they grew publicke, and (as coine crackt in exchange) corrupted: some of them both words and notes vnrespectiuely challenged by others. In regard of which wronges, though his selfe neglects these light fruits as superfluous blossomes of his deeper Studies, yet hath it pleased him vpon my entreaty, to grant me the impression of part of them.

This is a good statement of the characteristically non-professional attitude. Campion followed the Elizabethan custom of tossing off lyrics, sonnets, and ayres and allowing the manuscripts to float away on almost any breeze that might carry them to a friend. Apparently he had no highly developed sense of ownership. Even when the ayres were publicly abused, Campion does not seem to have protested to any extent. It was Rosseter who conscientiously gathered up what he could find and published them.

This carefree manner is again illustrated in the preface of *Two Bookes of Ayres* where Campion says that 'ovt of many Songs which, partly at the request of friends, partly for my owne recreation, were by mee long since composed, I haue now enfranchised a few, sending them forth diuided, according to their different subiect, into seuerall Bookes.' He concludes his remarks, saying: 'mine owne opinion of these Songs I deliuer thus:

> *Omnia nec nostria bona sunt, sed nec mala libris;*
> *Si placet hac cantes, hac quoque lege legas.'*

This quotation is sufficient to tell us that Campion scattered his songs at large, taking joy in their creation and revealing none of the pardonable pride that makes many desire to see work in print. Doubtless there are many of his ayres which are either lying unsigned in Elizabethan manuscripts or which have long since perished. Once more, at the beginning of the *Fourth Booke of Ayres*, that casual attitude is present. 'Some words are in these Bookes,' he says, 'which haue beene cloathed in Musicke by others, and I am content they then serued their turne; yet giue mee now leaue to make vse of mine owne. . . . To be briefe, all these Songs are mine, if you expresse them well, otherwise they are your owne. Farewell.' And Campion disarmed criticism, not only of this casual method of writing lyrics but also of the light-heartedness of his verse, by suggesting that critics who cavil over such things may have forgotten the times when

> *Loue and beautie, mirth and Musicke yeeld true ioyes,*
> *Though the* Cynickes *in their folly count them toyes.*

Campion's contemporary position as a true lyric poet was enviable. In the light of history, he stands out as one of the great figures in the English school of lutenist song-

writers which flourished so brilliantly in the first quarter
of the seventeenth century and whose work is still much
neglected. In the role of musical poet, he becomes an interesting figure in this golden age of the two arts in England. The examination of his unique position will, therefore, justify further the observation of Samuel Say, an
eighteenth-century writer, who pointed out that he
'who has the Address, or Felicity, to join These Two, the
Music I mean, and the *Power* of Numbers together, his
Works will be admir'd, wherever found. For This has
been the Practice of all those poets, whose Writings have
been the perpetual Admiration and Delight of their
Readers.'

IV

A BOOKE OF AYRES

IN 1601, two works appeared in England which definitely indicate the relationship of music and poetry at that time. The first of these was a collection of madrigals known as *The Triumphs of Oriana*; the second, *A Booke of Ayres, Set foorth to be song to the Lute, Orpherian, and Base Violl*, by Philip Rosseter, Lutenist, the first part of which contained ayres by Thomas Campion. The almost simultaneous appearance of these two works is significant in musical history on the one hand for marking the culmination of the English madrigal school, and on the other hand for marking the firm establishment of the English school of lutenist song-writers who introduced the fashion of singing ayres. From 1588 until sometime after 1601, the madrigal occupied the attention of the song-loving Elizabethans, while from 1597 to about 1617, the ayre, with its lute or other instrumental accompaniment, predominated. Fashions changed quickly in the Elizabethan period. In poetry, the sonnet was in vogue from 1590 to 1595. Then followed the ascendancy of the light lyric with two clearly defined periods: that of its association with music in the lyric song or ayre perfected by Campion; that of its independent literary development heralding the divorce of music and poetry towards the middle of the seventeenth century. In both music and poetry the tendency was toward simplification of form

54

and content. To understand the situation fully and to realize the strategic position in which Rosseter's *Booke of
Ayres* stands, it will be necessary to sketch the fashions
in music up to the time of its appearance.

The year 1588 so cleared the atmosphere that England,
free from the anxiety of outside dangers, was able to
settle down to a cultivation of the arts which it had neglected since the reign of Henry VIII. Except for the publication of Thomas Whythorne's songs in 1571, no collection of songs with music had been printed since 1530.
During this period, however, secular song in the form of
carols, catches, rounds, and ballads continued to enjoy
general acceptance. This music, which was distinctly
popular in character, has been recorded by Chappell in
his *Popular Music of the Olden Time*. As we have already
seen, the miscellanies also testify to the vogue. But
in 1588, two important publications stimulated interest in a type of secular song which was less popular
in character. The first of these was entitled *Psalmes,
Sonets, & songs of sadness and pietie, made into Musicke of
five parts: . . . By William Byrd, one of the Gent. of the
Queenes Maiesties honorable Chappell*; the second, *Musica
Transalpina*, published by Nicholas Yonge, an amateur
musician.

Byrd's work is thought to have been issued toward the
end of the previous year so that it actually preceded the
Musica Transalpina and thus gives another indication of
an interest in song during the middle of the sixteenth
century. It contained a preface beseeching the cultivation
of singing with the following 'reasons briefely set downe
by the auctor':

First, it is a knowledge easely taught, and quickly learned, wher ther is a good Master, & an apt Scoler.

2. The exercise of singing is delightful to Nature, and good to preserue the health of man.

3. It doth strengthen all parts of the brest, & doth open the pipes.

4. It is a singular good remedie for stutting and stamaring in the speech.

5. It is the best meanes to procure a perfect pronunciation, and to make a good Orator.

6. It is the onely way to know where Nature hath bestowed the benefit of a good voyce: which gift is so rare, as ther is not one among a thousand that hath it: & in many that excelent gift is lost, because they want art to expresse Nature.

7. Ther is not any Musicke of Instruments whatsoeuer, comparable to that which is made of the voyces of Men, wher the voices are good, & the same wel sorted and ordered.

8. The better the voyce is, the meeter it is to honour & serue God therewith: and the voice of man is chiefly to be imployed to that ende.

OMNIS SPIRITUS LAUDET DOMINUM

Since singing is so good a thing
I wish all men would learn to sing.

The fact that Byrd made a five-part arrangement of his songs indicates the general demand current at the time for group or part-singing. This was fashionable until succeeded by solo-singing which came in with the seventeenth century.

But the real impetus of the extraordinary outburst of madrigal music after 1588 is usually attributed to the *Musica Transalpina.* This was a collection of English translations of madrigals by Italian and Flemish com-

posers. Two madrigals by Byrd were also included.
Yonge advances the following reason for introducing this
hybrid work:

And albeit there be some English songs lately set forth by a
great master of music [Byrd], which for skill and sweetness
may content the most curious; yet because they are not many
in number, men delighted with variety, have wished more
of the same sort: for whose cause chiefly I endeavored to get
into my hands all such English songs as were praise worthy,
and, amongst others, I had the hap to find in the hands of
some of my good friends, certain Italian Madrigals, translated,
most of them, five years ago, by a gentleman for his private
delight . . . and finding the same to be singularly well liked,
not only of those for whose cause I gathered them, but of
many skilful gentlemen and other great musicians . . . I
was so bold . . . as to entreat the rest . . . I kept them . . .
for a long time by me, not presuming to put my sickle in
another man's corn, till such time as I heard, that the same
being dispersed into many men's hands, were by some persons
altogether unknown to the owner like to be published in
print, which made me adventure to set this work in hand.

From this it is clear again that interest in song had been
manifested previous to these publications.

The appearance of *Musica Transalpina* served as a sig-
nal to release the general desire for musical expression and
by 1630, some eighty-eight collections of madrigals alone
had been published. The Italian influence is, of course,
strongly indicated in this madrigal fashion; but in England, it only served as an impetus to self-expression. Outside forces have been needed on many occasions, but
English tradition adapts foreign forms quickly to English
moulds. The English madrigal school was the result.
When Yonge brought out his second set of madrigals in

1597, because of the 'gracious acceptance of my first one,' the English had absorbed the form, and numerous collections by English composers appeared in quick succession.

The effect of this collection on English poetry can only be suggested. The English translations of the Italian words were of a pedestrian nature. As a result, English composers began to search for English poems which might lend themselves to the requirements of polyphonic music. A definite demand for short, concise lyrics was created and the poets, recognizing the situation, complied. Thus the fashion of writing poems with the definite idea of having them set to music or suitable for musical settings, conditioned the Elizabethan lyric.

The Triumphs of Oriana, published in 1601 by the famous musician, Thomas Morley, represented the pinnacle of the madrigal fashion. It consisted of twenty-five madrigals in praise of Queen Elizabeth with the last lines of each poem based on the common refrain:

> *Then sang the shepherds and Nymphs of Diana*
> *Long live Fair Oriana*

Twenty-three composers were represented, while several other prominent musicians, among them William Byrd, were conspicuous by their absence. From this collection of madrigals arises one significant fact: the indication of the prevalence of secular music, and its predominance over the motet style of sacred music to which the prominent composers of the day had devoted their attention. Thomas Morley looked askance at this shift of taste:

Such be the new fangled opinions of our countrey men, who will highlie esteem whatsoeuer commeth from beyond the seas, and specially from *Italie*, be it neuer so simple, contemning that which is done at home though it be neuer so excellent. Nor yet is that fault of esteeming so highlie the light Musicke particular to vs in England, but general through the world: which is the cause that the musitions in all countreyes and chiefely in *Italy*, haue imploied most of their studies in it: whereupon learned men of our time writing vpon *Cicero* his dreame of *Scipio* saith; that the musicians of this age, instead of drawing the minds of men to the consideration of heauen and heauenlie things, doe by the contrarie set wide open the gates of hell, causing such as delight in the exercise of their art to tumble headlong into perdition.

He thought, however, that the madrigal was the best kind of secular or light music of the period since 'use sheweth that it is a kind of Musicke made vpon songs and sonnets, such as *Petrarcha* and manie Poets of our time haue excelled in . . . As for the Musicke it is next vnto the Motet the most articifial [artistic], and to men of vnderstanding, most delightful.'

The madrigal was a polyphonic composition for two or more voices singing unaccompanied. Each voice-part followed a melodic line related to the melodic material of the other voice-parts yet of equal interest and importance in itself. The words, grouped in short phrases which were repeated several times, were sung by the different voices one after another in fugal fashion. The result was a confusion of the sense of the words but a riot of musical rhythm and melody.

In addition to the madrigal, there were other kinds of light music such as canzonets, or little short songs, which were in musical treatment a counterfeit of the madrigal. Still lighter were the ballets, or dances, 'songs, which being song to a dittie may likewise be daunced: these and all other kinds of light Musicke sauing the Madrigal, are by a generall name called ayres. There be also another kind of Ballets commonlie called *fa las*.' And added to all this vocal music was a mass of instrumental music asserting itself more and more during the period.

Through all this polyphonic period, the charm of a single melody, lost for the moment in the maze of many voices, nevertheless continued to exist. If it was accompanied at all, that accompaniment was probably in unison with the melody. It may be found in the songs of the pre-Shakespearean drama. In vocal polyphony, the music had become more important than the words though the meaning of the words might often have been the source of inspiration for flowery musical phrases. But for stage use, where the words were equally important with the music, the intricacies of polyphonic music were unsatisfactory. Thus the song with a single melody persevered during the madrigal fashion under the protection of the drama. When the popularity of the madrigals abated, an interesting change took place. The vocal melody came into its own again and the polyphonic writing of the madrigals became metamorphosed into an accompaniment of harmonic chords. This accompaniment was played by the instruments which had gradually attained a recognized place in Elizabethan music in spite of the popularity of vocal music.

Such, in brief, is the story of the development of the 'ayre' which is, in its purest form, a melody with an instrumental accompaniment. Until 1601, the influence of the madrigal was so strong that the ayres were usually written as part-songs. Byrd's *Psalmes, Sonets, and songs* written for five parts, revealed the influence of the demand for this type. In his epistle to the reader, however, Byrd remarked: 'Heere are diuers songs, which being originally made for Instruments to expresse the harmonie, and one voyce to pronounce the dittie, are now framed in all parts for voyces to sing the same.' The tendency toward the simpler form of the ayre had appeared before 1588. It blossomed forth, however, with John Dowland's *First Booke of Songs or Ayres* in 1597. Secular music now entered a different channel and for twenty years or so the ayre was the fashion.

A glance at a madrigal and an ayre at once reveals the important transition which took place. In place of the contrapuntal music written for voices alone, there is a solo melody with an instrumental accompaniment based on a simple harmonic scheme of chord progression. The instrument was usually a lute. Madrigals were printed without bar lines in part-books so that the whole score was rarely available and the full effect was gained only in performance. Ayres were printed in one book: the solo and lute accompaniment placed on one page, the optional part-song arrangement on the opposite page in such a way that a single copy answered for the singers standing in a semi-circle. When there was no part-song arrangement and the ayre was presented in its pure form, only the format of a single page was used. Bar lines were introduced as an aid for keeping the voice and the accompaniment together. A *Booke of Ayres* was, of course, printed in this fashion. The words for the madrigal were usually confined to a single stanza while the ayre had several stanzas. In quality, the words of the ayre were generally far superior because its form threw the words into sharp relief and made them equally important with the music. Campion's importance consists in his having struck a perfect balance between the two.

The ayre may be said to represent the decline of vocal polyphony in that it reduces the multiple melodies of the madrigal to a single melody and marks the transition in which the importance of vocal music *per se* was waning and that of instrumental music was rising. The two meet curiously balanced in this form. Finally, the ayre reveals the ground on which music and poetry stood with equal footing before they proceeded along their independent ways acquiring characteristics that widened the gap at every step. The verses once written for or with music attained a new significance. They became literature. But the secret of their charm is linked to the music with which they were associated.

When John Dowland, famous at home and abroad as the greatest of lutenists, published his *First Booke of Songs or Ayres* in 1597, he laid the foundations of the modern art-song which, as we have seen, was later perfected by Schubert, Schumann, Brahms, Franz, and Wolf. Though he made a concession to the popular demand in allowing a part-song arrangement to be published, nevertheless he maintained his principle of having the chief melodic interest in the upper voice. Campion had a similar experience which he recorded in his preface to *Two Bookes of Ayres* thus:

These Ayres were for the most part framed at first for one voyce with the Lute, or Violl, but vpon occasion they haue since been filled with more parts, which who so please may vse, who like not may leaue. Yet doe wee daily obserue, that when any shall sing a Treble to an Instrument, the standers by will be offring at an inward part out of their owne nature; and, true or false, out it must, though to the peruerting of the whole harmonie.

Dowland, of course, did not originate the idea for Byrd had planned to use it before him and it was part of the evolutionary process. But Dowland devoted all his energies to this one form of expression, and in it attained immortality equal to that of his nineteenth-century descendants. His books of ayres launched the English school of lutenist song-writers on a brilliant though brief career.

The following year Michael Cavendish published a book of ayres and madrigals in which fourteen of the songs were without any alternative setting for part singing. Robert Jones published his *Booke of Ayres* in 1601, also omitting the part-song arrangements. He effected a new fashion by adding an alternative accompaniment for the bass viol in a special tuning. But whether his book preceded or followed the Rosseter-Campion collection of the same year is not at present determinable, and of little importance.

The significance of the publication of the Rosseter-Campion *Booke of Ayres* cannot be over-emphasized. In the first place, it is important for definitely establishing the ayre as Dowland conceived it in its pure form of a solo melody with lute accompaniment. Secondly, it marks the ascendancy of the light lyric to the highest point in Elizabethan lyrical poetry. And finally, it announces the appearance of Thomas Campion as a musical poet.

As we have seen, the madrigal reached the pinnacle of fashion in 1601 and Dowland used the new art form of the ayre in 1597. Campion was well aware of Dowland's procedure for he had written an epigram which was prefixed to Dowland's *First Booke of Songs or Ayres*. The dedication of the Rosseter-Campion work reveals that Campion began writing ayres long before the publication of them in conjunction with Rosseter. He had composed them during his idle hours and distributed them freely to his friends. According to the preface, *A Booke of Ayres* represents the gathering of some of these scattered compositions. Just as the appearance of the *Musica Transalpina* in 1588 had stimulated the writing of madrigals, so the Rosseter-Campion collection in 1601 crystallized the form of the ayre. This new form of song was most suitable for masques and plays and satisfactory to patrons of the theatres who demanded songs and dances in the drama. Dowland's famous *Lachrimae* is, of course, the classic example of a song which was arranged for such occasions. The fashion of the ayre was, therefore, in full swing by 1601.

The preface to *A Booke of Ayres* is so important in defining this form, that it must be quoted almost in full:

What Epigrams are in Poetrie, the same are Ayres in musicke, then in their chiefe perfection when they are short and well seasoned. But to clogg a light song with a long Praeludium, is to corrupt the nature of it. Manie rests in Musicke were inuented either for necessitie of the fuge, or granted as an harmonicall licence in songs of many parts: but in Ayres I find no vse they haue, vnlease it be to make a vulgar and triuiall modulation seeme to the ignorant strange and to the iudiciall tedious. A naked Ayre without guide, or prop, or

colour but his owne, is easily censured of euerie eare, and
requires so much the more inuention to make it please. And
as *Martiall* speakes in defence of his short Epigrams, so may
I say in th'apologie of Ayres, that where there is a full volume,
there can be no imputation of shortnes. The Lyricke Poets
among the Greekes and Latines were first inuenters of Ayres,
tying themselues strictly to the number, and the value of their
sillables, of which sort, you shall find here onely one song
in Saphicke verse; the rest are after the fascion of the time,
eare-pleasing rimes without Arte. The subject of them is
for the most part, amorous, and why not amorous songs, as
well as amorous attires? Or why not new Ayres, as well as
new fascions? For the Note and Tableture, if they satisfie
the most, we haue our desire, let expert masters please themselues with better. And if anie light error hath escaped vs, the
skilfull may easily correct it, the vnskilfull will hardly per-
ceiue it . . . nevertheless, as in Poesie we giue the prehemi-
nence to the Heroicall Poeme, so in Musicke we yeeld the
chiefe place to the graue, and well inuented Motet, but not
to euery harsh and dull confused Fantasie where in multitude
of points the Harmonie is quite drowned. Ayres haue both
their Art and pleasure, and I will conclude of them, as the
Poet did in his censure, of *Catvllvs*, the Lyricke, and *Vergil*
the Heroicke writer:

> *Tantum magna suo debet Verona Catullo:*
> *Quantum parua suo Mantua Vergilio.*

No definite clues to the authorship of this document
are available. Whether Rosseter, who was a close friend
of Campion, gleaned these thoughts from him or whether
he persuaded Campion to write the address is a matter
for speculation. The style strongly suggests that Campion may have been the author. Certain ideas—for instance, that of the poetical analogy of the ayres, or the

references to the Latin poets—are paralleled in the address to the reader of his *Two Bookes of Ayres*. But this similarity of statement is not conclusive evidence of the authorship.

The preface is, of course, most important for the spontaneous use of poetical analogy to define the ayre. Campion does not call his poems lyrics, nor with their musical settings does he call them only songs. Following in the tradition of the lyrical poets among the Greeks and Romans, he calls them 'ayres' because they represent the marriage of music and poetry. He says later, in the preface to *Two Bookes of Ayres*, that 'short Ayres, if they be skilfully framed, and naturally exprest, are like quicke and good Epigrammes in Poesie, many of them shewing as much artifice, and breeding as great difficultie as a larger Poeme.' The same idea is expressed in the preface quoted above, thus: 'What Epigrams are in Poetrie, the same are Ayres in musicke, then in their chiefe perfection when they are short and well seasoned.' This comparison of an ayre with an epigram is an ingenious stroke, especially since, in the following sentences commenting on the form of the ayre, the writer states that it should have neither prelude nor epilogue. As a complete entity of words and music in itself, the ayre is impressively short. Campion as a miniaturist attained his effects by simplicity and directness in both mediums. The ayres are also equally well-seasoned. If the words have an epigrammatic sting, then the music is correspondingly spicy. Yet the sting of an epigram is often mitigated by the influence of the music so that the result is an ineffably charming creation.

Reference is made to 'eare-pleasing rimes without Arte.' The meaning is probably that in comparison with lyrics in classical meter, of which there is one in Sapphic verse in the collection, these light lyrics show no particular art in construction. The ayre is here regarded as a new fashion thus giving *A Booke of Ayres* its rightful place beside *The Triumphs of Oriana*. In referring to the tablature, the writer means, of course, the lute accompaniment. This was not written in notes but indicated in letters on a staff to signify the position and the string to be used in securing a particular chord. A glance at the reproduction of the original ayres shows that the lute tablature was placed below the line of melody with the rhythm specially indicated in a formula printed directly above.

The fact is also recorded in this document that ayres have their art. In comparison with the complexities of the contrapuntal writing in the madrigals and motets, the art of writing ayres may seem comparatively simple. Morley looked on a mastery of the technique of the motet as the height of achievement for a composer. But the attainment of the simplicity which is characteristic of ayres is also an art. To find the right musical phrase to fit a word-phrase is far more difficult than it appears to be. Anyone who doubts this will soon understand the subtleties involved by attempting to combine words and music. A successful combination comes from a control over the technique of both arts, and there are few modern song-writers who approach the happy union of words and music.

A Booke of Ayres contains forty-two songs, twenty-one

of which are by Campion, twenty-one by Rosseter. Usually the lutenists' books contained about twenty-one ayres, but this 'two-faced *Ianus* thus in one bodie vnited' is unique in this respect. The evidence for Campion's authorship of words and music in the first part of the book lies in the dedication where Rosseter states that

the first ranke of songs are of his owne composition, made at his vacant houres, and priuately emparted to his friends whereby they grew both publicke, and (as coine crackt in exchange) corrupted: some of them both words and notes vnrespectiuely challenged by others. In regard of which wronges, though his selfe neglects these light fruits as superfluous blossomes of his deeper Studies, yet hath it pleased him, vpon my entreaty, to grant me the impression of part of them, to which I haue added an equall number of mine owne.

He had evidently written these ayres prior to 1601—in all probability choosing the pure form of the ayre as the form which most appealed to him. In doing this he may be ranked among the pioneers of the new fashion. But the reason for the unique size of the book is given in Rosseter's statement that he had gathered some of Campion's songs 'to which I have added an equall number of mine owne.' Contrary to general supposition, there is nothing here to indicate that Campion was the author of the words of this part. If Campion had written them, it would seem natural that Rosseter might have mentioned the fact since the whole tone of the dedication is a precise statement of the circumstances of publication. Furthermore, the irregular and sometimes inferior quality of the ayres in this second part gives an impression of authorship other than that of Campion. He may have contributed some of the lyrics, but in view of the fact that he generally wrote both words and music together, it seems unnecessary to include this section of *A Booke of Ayres* in his works until a more definite identification is made. To believe that Rosseter might have composed words and music as Campion did is quite possible. The customary practice of the times indicates such a possibility, and the wording of the dedication inclines toward this interpretation. The important fact, however, is that at least in Part I the words and music were the work of Campion. This allows an insight into the relationship of the music and poetry hitherto unavailable. Campion's own publications, in which he admits the relationship is close, offer further opportunity.

The direct bearing on poetry of the simplification of the music to the form of the ayre was that it threw the words into a position of greater importance than was possible in the madrigal. With both the words and music on an equal footing, attention to the words became all the more significant. This circumstance probably influenced the poets to produce more exquisite lyrics. Incidentally, the majority of Shakespeare's songs were written shortly after the change of style recorded above. So the 1601 *Booke of Ayres* has the added significance of marking the ascendancy of the Elizabethan lyric in a period when music was its source of inspiration. In the works of Robert Herrick and the other Cavaliers who represent the last of the songsters in the period that followed lie the echoes of this influence. The literary characteristics of this later type of song are too familiar to dwell upon. It is sufficient to point out that this 1601 collection of ayres is part of the foundation on which the seventeenth-century lyric was built.

Finally *A Booke of Ayres* focuses attention on Thomas Campion as a musical poet. Because he composed both the words of his lyrics and the music of his songs, he attained the highest point in the art of song composition in this age. Davey comments on the ayres in an interesting fashion, concluding 'that, as a rule, the poems and the music were simultaneously conceived; I ground this belief on the detailed parallelism in the metre of the successive stanzas in the Ayres, through which the same music easily fits them all.'

As a practical musician, Campion effected the perfect union of words and notes. The full charm of this relationship in the ayres can be appreciated only when they are considered in their original settings. When read, the lyrics, however refreshing and delightful they may be, are nevertheless incomplete without the musical setting. The music brings an added daintiness, a resonant melody, and, most significant of all, a series of little changes in meanings and subtle connotations. Campion was an individualistic artist whose fastidious taste in the combination of words and notes brought to his ayres a certain grace and rare sense of perfection that is the particular characteristic of all Elizabethan song and, of course, the secret of its spontaneity.

V

THE POET'S ART OF ENGLISH POESY

IN his *Observations in the Art of English Poesy* published in 1602, Campion proposed to 'induce a true forme of versefying into our language.' His treatise was, in a sense, an answer to the second part of a wish expressed by William Webbe in his *Discourse of English Poetrie* of 1586 that 'some perfect platforme or Prosodia of versifying were by them [the poets] ratified and sette downe, eyther in immitation of Greekes and Latines, or, where it would skant abyde the touch of theyr Rules, the like obseruations selected and established by the naturall affection of the speeche.'

That Campion made no attempt to justify the adaptation of English poetry to classical forms of prosody, as some earlier Elizabethans had tried to do, is clearly stated on the title page of the *Observations* which calls attention 'wherein it is demonstratiuely prooued, and by example confirmed, that the English toong will receiue eight seuerall kinds of numbers, proper to it selfe, which are all in this booke set forth, and were neuer before this time by any man attempted.' His interest was in English numbers—numbers that could be fashioned out of the English language and be perfect in themselves without rime as an additional ornament. In promoting this interest, Campion treated some of his material so concisely that his brevity has resulted in obscurity and confusion

71

for modern critics. He furthermore appealed to the classics for example. This was a natural attitude for him though again the significance of the appeal has been misconstrued. Writing in 1602, Campion had a whole tradition of Elizabethan criticism behind him and his knowledge had been gathered over a long period of study and observation. Consciously or unconsciously he had absorbed many of his predecessors' ideas and suggestions. To cite the authors that he might have consulted on the particular points in the *Observations*, however, would be as difficult as it would be dangerous. Writers borrowed freely from one another in this age, each succeeding author profiting by the conclusions of the last. Campion's treatise, in the opinion of the noted authority on English metrics, T.S.Omond, is, for these reasons, considered the best of the Elizabethan critical essays.

Elizabethan criticism arose among the more learned men of the time—men such as Roger Ascham, Gabriel Harvey, and Sir Philip Sidney—out of a discontent with the low estate of poetry, and the consequent desire for change. In the true Elizabethan spirit, the ambitions of these early critics were most extravagant. They desired nothing short of perfection. Poetry, they had learned from the classical study, was of divine origin. Thomas Lodge in 1579 said that 'Poetrye commeth from aboue, from a heauenly seate of a glorious God, vnto an excellent creature man.' The poet's position was an exalted one. 'Poetes were the first raysors of cities, prescribers of good lawes, mayntayners of religion, disturbors of the wicked, aduancers of the wel disposed, inuentors of laws, and lastly the very fot-path to knowledge and vnder-standing.' But such was neither the condition of poets nor the place of poesy in the early decades of Elizabeth's reign. Swarms of ballad-mongers, 'the rude multitude of rusticall Rymers' turned out endless riff-raff called verse, which had little to commend it. Most of this versifying is not extant. Though such verse might be worthless *per se*, an appreciable amount of it would probably help critics to understand the attitude of those Elizabethans who felt that something had to be done to change the conditions. As Sidney said: there was 'iust cause to make a pittiful defence of poore Poetry, which from almost the highest estimation of learning is fallen to be the laughing-stocke of children.' Out of this degenerate state of po-etry, then, came a desire for perfection.

With this in mind, the Elizabethan critics entered a paradoxical campaign against the lot of common poetry. Their ideal may have been aptly expressed in the work of a foreigner, King James VI of Scotland, who wrote a 'Sonnet Decifring The Perfyte Poete' in 1584.

> *Ane rype ingyne, ane quick and walkned witt,*
> *With sommair reasons, suddenlie applyit,*
> *For euery purpose vsing reasons fitt,*
> *With skilfulnes, where learning may be spyit,*
> *With pithie wordis, for to expres yow by it*
> *His full intention in his proper leid,*
> *The puritie quhairof weill hes he tryit,*
> *With memorie to keip quwhat he dois reid,*
> *With skilfulnes and figuris, quhilks proceid*
> *From* Rhetorique, *with euerlasting fame,*

With vthers woundring, preassing with all speid
For to atteine to merite sic a name:
All thir into the perfyte Poëte be.
Goddis, grant I may obteine the Laurell trie.

This goal of perfection, however, was sought through
various avenues of approach. Some authors revived the
medieval tradition; others made experiments in adapting
the verse forms from the medieval Latin; still others—
such as the humanists, Ascham, Harvey, Sidney, and
Campion—turned to classical Latin for their models.

A discussion of humanism as a revival of interest in
classical life and in classical literature is not necessary
here. The ideal was the classical past as seen through the
Elizabethan imagination. The attitude was that everything native appeared barbarous and should therefore be
refined according to ideal standards. Ascham expressed
the humanistic position in a familiar passage too important not to quote again:

This matter maketh me gladly remember my sweete tyme
spent at Cambrige, and the pleasant talke which I had oft
with M. *Cheke* and M. *Watson* of this fault, not onely in the
olde Latin Poets, but also in our new English Rymers at this
day. They wished as *Virgil* and *Horace* were not wedded to
follow the faultes of former fathers . . . but by right *Imita-*
tion of the perfit Grecians had brought Poetrie to perfitnesse
also in the Latin tong, that we Englishmen likewise would
acknowledge and vnderstand rightfully our rude beggerly
ryming, brought first into Italie by *Gothes* and *Hunnes* whan
all good verses and all good learning to were destroyd by
them, and after caryed into France and Germanie, and at last
receyued into England by men of excellent wit in deede, but

of small learning and lesse iudgement in that behalfe. But now, when men know the difference, and haue the examples, both of the best and of the worst, surelie to follow rather the *Gothes* in Ryming than the *Greekes* in trew versifiyng were euen to eate ackornes with swyne, when we may freely eate wheate bread emonges men.

The position was justified. To the Elizabethan who looked about London, imperial Rome was the ideal; the customs of classical civilization were therefore the ideal.

But before attaining this perfection in poetry which had sunk so low, rules for restraint, proportion, and symmetry were needed. Thus there arose a desire for discipline. This second desire brought another cause of discontent. No order in poetry could be achieved until the chaotic state of English orthography had been put in order.

I am of Opinion [said Gabriel Harvey writing to Edmund Spenser] there is no one more regular and justifiable direction, eyther for the assured and infallible Certaintie of our English Artificiall Prosodye particularly, or generally to bring our Language into Arte and to frame a Grammar or Rhetoricke thereof, than first of all vniversally to agree upon *one and the same Orthographie,* in all pointes conformable and proportionate to our *Common Natural Prosodye.*

Such a desire for discipline as this procedure required, led to much confusion when any observance of quantity in verse was demanded. But the chaotic state of English orthography was never set in order during the period of Elizabethan criticism. The desire for discipline did not coincide with the Elizabethan temperament. Campion, writing on quantity, appeared as confused as his contemporaries who adjusted spelling and fixed the quantity of words more or less arbitrarily in a spirit of compromise.

The concentrated attack of the critics was against rime and rimers. Ascham began it in the quotation given above. He pointed out, however, that

this mislikyng of Ryming beginneth not now of any new-fangle singularitie, but hath bene long misliked of many, and that of men of greatest learnyng and deepest iudgement. And soch that defend it do so, either for lacke of knowledge what is best, or els of verie enuie that any should performe that in learnyng, whereunto they, as I sayd before, either for ignorance can not, or for idlenes will not, labor to attaine vnto.

The general feeling was vented by 'E.K.' in *The Epistle Dedicatory to the Shepheards Calendar*: 'I scorne and spue out the rakehellye route of our ragged rymers . . . which without learning boste, without iudgement iangle, without reason rage and fome, as if some instinct of Poeticall spirite had newly rauished them aboue the meanenesse of commen capacitie.' William Webbe, inclined toward rime, wished to pass over 'the vncountable rabble of ryming Ballet makers and compylers of sencelesse sonets,' otherwise

euery one that can frame a Booke in Ryme, though for want of matter it be but in commendations of Copper noses or Bottle Ale, wyll catch at the Garlande due to Poets; whose potticall, poeticall (I should say), heades I would wyshe at their wor-shipfull commencements might in steede of Lawrell be gor-giously garnished with faire greene Barley in token of their good affection to our Englishe malt.

All this development of criticism with these three dominant motifs—the desire for perfection, the desire for

discipline, and the desire to correct the abuse of rime—
happened before 1590. Campion does not treat this traditional background elaborately. He states his conception
of Poetry in his dedication as follows: 'Poesy in all kind
of speaking is the chiefe beginner, and maintayner of eloquence, not only helping the eare with the acquaintance
of sweet [ideal] numbers, but also raysing the minde to a
more high and lofty conceite.' It is in the second chapter
of the *Observations* that the traditional ideas appear
though they are thrown together in some confusion.
The chapter is devoted to 'declaring the vnaptnesse of
Rime in Poesie.' In the following quotation it may be deduced that Campion has succinctly summarized the whole
tenor of Elizabethan criticism.

I am not ignorant that whosoeuer shall by way of repre-
hension examine the imperfections of Rime must encounter
with many glorious enemies, and those very expert and ready
at their weapon, that can if neede be extempore . . . rime a
man to death. Besides there is growne a kind of prescription
in the vse of Rime, to forestall the right of true numbers,
as also the consent of many nations, against all which it
may seeme a thing almost impossible and vaine to contend.
*All this and more can not yet deterre me from a lawful defence of
perfection, or make me any whit the sooner adheare to that which is
lame and vnbeseeming.* For custome I alleage that ill vses are
to be abolisht, and that things naturally imperfect can not
be perfected by vse. Old customes, if they be better, why should
they not be recald, as the yet florishing custome of numerous
poesy vsed among the *Romanes* and *Grecians*? But the vnaptnes
of our toongs and the difficultie of imitation dishartens vs:
againe the facilitie and popularitie of Rime creates as many
Poets, as a hot sommer flies . . . But the noble *Grecians*
and *Romaines*, whose skilfull monuments outliue barbarisme,

tyed themselues to the strict obseruation of poeticall numbers, so abandoning the childish titillation of riming.

Campion had no quarrel with rime *per se*. Rime, he stated in the same chapter, 'ought . . . sparingly to be vs'd least it should offend the eare with tedious affectation.' It was the current abuse of rime that vexed him. More serious than this, however, was the fact that the multitude of rimers, who found the writing of verse so easy because of rime, were not keeping the right proportions in their verses. They used rime to conceal defects. Campion, therefore, found fault with rimers for writing such lines as

Was it my desteny or dismall chaunce,

because they made the line 'to fall out shorter than it ought by nature.' The line *appears* to be a five-foot, ten-syllable line. It *sounds* short of the five feet which it is supposed to have. But when the line is divided into feet, it will be found that the last two syllables of *desteny* are used for a whole foot. Campion maintained that since these were short syllables, they did not equal an iambus or trochee in sound-value, therefore the line was wanting in metrical equivalence. The caesura after *desteny* does not affect the meter of the verse. No matter how long a pause is made the *sound* of the line is not equalled to one containing five balanced feet. Thus there is a 'confus'd inequalitie of sillables' in this line. He found still

another fault in Rime altogether intollerable, which is, that it inforceth a man oftentimes to abiure his matter and extend a short conceit beyond all bounds of arte; for in *Quatorzens* [sonnets], methinks, the poet handles his subiect as tyranically as *Procrustes* the thiefe his prisoners, whom, when he had taken, he vsed to cast vpon a bed, which if they were too short to fill, he would stretch them longer, if too long, he would cut them shorter.

That Campion has made an important observation will be readily grasped by anyone who is familiar with the conceits of Elizabethan poetry.

These, then, were Campion's remarks on the abuse of rime. He treated the whole subject in a rather cursory and altogether too brief manner. But his interest lay in the eight kinds of *English* numbers which he wished to introduce into the language. To these he devoted considerable space 'for the vulgar and vnarteficiall custome of riming hath, I know, deter'd many excellent wits from the exercise of English Poesy.' Yet it is because of his remarks on rime that Campion's *Observations* are usually remembered. The reason for this is the protest registered by his contemporary Samuel Daniel.

The appearance of the *Observations* was apparently the cause of great distress to Daniel:

We are tolde how that our measures goe wrong, all Ryming is grosse, vulgare, barbarous; which if it be so, we haue lost much labour to no purpose; and, for mine owne particular, I cannot but blame the fortune of the times and mine owne Genius that cast me vppon so wrong a course, drawne with the current of custome, and an vnexamined example . . . But yet now, vpon the great discouery of these new measures, threatning to ouerthrow the whole state of Ryme in this kingdom, I must either stand out to defend, or els be forced to forsake my selfe and giue ouer all . . . We could well haue allowed of his numbers, had he not disgraced our Ryme, which both Custome and Nature doth most powerfully defend.

So Daniel justified himself in his well-known *Defence of Ryme*.

Why was Daniel's alarm so great? There seem to be two reasons for this. The first reflects the reputable contemporary position of Campion himself. Daniel said that he 'is a man of faire parts, and good reputation; and therefore the reproach forcibly cast from such a hand may throw downe more at once then the labors of many shall in long time build vp againe, specially vpon the slippery foundation of opinion, and the world's inconstancy.' A reproach from such a source as Thomas Campion, then, was considered important. Again, Daniel pointed out that if Campion had not disparaged rimers, they 'would haue bin glad to haue stood quietly by him, and perhaps commended his aduenture.' 'Me thinkes,' he continues further on, 'it is a strange imperfection that men should ouer-runne the estimation of good things with so violent a censure, as though it must please none else, because it likes not them.' There was still another reason. Such a suggestion as a scheme of new numbers without rime— which could mean either quantitative verse, or merely blank verse—would be 'wrong to *England*, in seeking to lay reproach vpon her natiue ornaments, and to turne the faire streame and full course of her accents into the shallow current of a lesse vncertaintie, cleane out of the way of her knowne delight. Campion thus threatened to mar the glory of England by suggesting quantitative verse without rime, and in England's name, Samuel Daniel was come to the rescue.

So admirable and so well received was Daniel's *Defence of Ryme* that he appears to have spoken the last word on

the subject for the Elizabethans. Campion remained
silent after Daniel's pamphlet was published. There was
never more than one edition of the *Observations*. But because he chose to use rime to perfection in the ayres that
he wrote thereafter, the argument has been advanced
that Campion was converted by Daniel. That is possibly
so. There is reason to believe, nevertheless, that Campion
only added rime to his numbers. The fact that he is noted
for an unusual variety of meter in his poems, so much so
that he has been called a 'curious metrist,' seems sufficient evidence for such a suggestion. Further proof lies in
the musical settings of his ayres where the rime of the
words can be of only secondary importance, while the
cadence of a line of verse and music together are of prime
significance. From this point of view, which is creative,
rime has little influence on the cadence or rhythm of a
line. 'For rhyme may help the *reader* to catch the poet's
melody and yet have no place in the formation of that
melody. It communicates the cadence to the reader rather
than determines it for the poet.' Though Campion never
stated his *general* attitude toward rime, he implied such
an interpretation. An examination of his practice, which
is reserved for a later chapter, bears this out. The attitude was probably not unlike that expressed by John Milton in his preface to *Paradise Lost*. Milton, who like
Campion wrote beautiful rimes, said that rime is

No necessary adjunct or true ornament of poem or good verse,
in longer works especially, but the invention of a barbarous
age, to set off wretched matter and lame metre; graced indeed
since by the use of some famous modern poets, carried away
by custom, but much to their own vexation, hindrance, and

constraint to express many things otherwise, and for the most part worse, than else they would have expressed them. Not without cause therefore some both Italian and Spanish poets of prime note have rejected rime both in longer and shorter works . . . as a thing of itself, to all judicious ears, trivial and of no true musical delight; which consists only in apt numbers, fit quantity of syllables, and the sense variously drawn out from one verse into another, not in the jingling sound of like endings . . . a fault avoided by the learned ancients both in poetry and all good oratory. This neglect then of rime so little is to be taken for a defect, though it may seem so perhaps to vulgar readers, that it rather is to be esteemed an example set, the first in English, of ancient liberty recovered to heroic poem from the troublesome and modern bondage of riming.

The answer to the question of Campion's silence appears to lie in the *Observations* themselves. The poem at the beginning of the treatise shows his attitude:

> *Alas, poore booke, I rue*
> *Thy rash selfe-loue; Goe, spread thy pap'ry wings:*
> *Thy lightnes cannot helpe or hurt my fame.*

It is also well known that his ayres were products of his lighter moments. Furthermore, that Campion fully realized what he was doing was clearly outlined in the opening sentence of his second chapter where he said he expected to encounter many adversaries, but that nevertheless he would develop his theories of poetry. His position is strengthened near the end of the ninth chapter where he stated that 'some eares accustomed altogether to the fatnes of rime may perhaps except against the cadences of these numbers [inflections at the close of a line]; but let

any man iudicially examine them, and he shall finde they
close of themselues so perfectly that the help of rime were
not only in them superfluous but also absurd.' Campion
was interested, therefore, not so much in rime as in the
delicate balance of numbers themselves.

Upon close examination of Greek and Latin verse,
Campion found that it was generally distinguished by
only three feet: the dactyl, the iambus, and the trochee.
Spondees, tribrachs, and anapests 'are but *as seruants to
these*' while 'diuers other feete I know are by the Grammarians cited *but to little purpose.*' The question was
whether these feet would agree with the nature of English syllables. Campion rejected the dactyl as 'unfit for
our vse' since

the *Heroicall* verse that is distinguished by the *Dactile* hath
bene oftentimes attempted in our English toong, but with
passing pitifull successe; and no wonder, seeing it is an attempt altogether against the nature of our language. For both
the concurse of our monosillables make our verses vnapt to
slide, and also, if we examine our polysillables, we shall finde
few of them, by reason of their heauiness, willing to serue in
place of a *Dactile*.

Ascham had realized the unfitness of the dactyl when he
pointed out that 'our English tong, hauing in vse chiefly
wordes of one syllable which commonly be long, doth
not well receiue the nature of *Carmen Heroicum*, bicause
dactylus.'

But Campion found that the iambic feet 'fall out so
naturally in our toong, that, if we examine our owne
writers, we shall find they vnawares hit oftentimes vpon
the true *Iambick* numbers.' Ascham and Gascoigne had

recognized the special fitness of the iambic foot and Gascoigne lamented that it was the only foot used in English rimes. Furthermore, Campion showed that the '*Trochaick foote*, which is but an *Iambick* turn'd ouer and ouer, must of force in like manner accord in proportion with our Brittish sillables and so produce an English *Trochaicall* verse.' Having, then, two kinds of verses demonstrable in the English language, it might be possible to derive others from these. Thus Campion prepared the way for the introduction of his scheme of the eight kinds of English verses which he considered proper for English poetry.

The first kind of verse was, of course, the iambic pentameter, the 'most naturall and auncient English verse.' But a variation of it, the 'Iambick licentiate,' illustrated by the line,

> *Harke how these winds | do | murmure at thy flight*,

was something different. Campion conceived its structure as follows:

an *Iambick* in the third place . . . that the forepart of the verse may the gentler slide into his *Dimeter* . . . *Hark how these winds*, there the voice naturally affects a rest; then *murmur at thy flight*, that is of itselfe a perfect number [Campion calls it *Dimeter* and makes it his second kind of verse] . . . and therefore the other odde sillable betweene them ought to be short, least the verse should hang too much betweene the naturall pause of the verse, and the *Dimeter* following; the which *Dimeter* though it be naturally *Trochaical*, yet it seemes to haue his originall out of the *Iambick* verse.

The term licentiate seems to infer that the line, though iambic pentameter, can be made up of other feet besides iambics. By substituting trochees, spondees, or tribrachs except in the third place—a whole series of subtle variations within the range of a poet's own ability and invention are allowed. The subtlety of this observation rests in Campion's ability to think in feet and *hear* in verses or verse-phrases. The admission of the tribrach into his verse is a real contribution for his time. Three syllables may be equal to the sound of two—iambics or trochees. Here, then, was a verse which was a variation of Gascoigne's 'sole foot' line. Finally, and this is most important, Campion pointed out that 'no man is tyed altogether to obserue this rule [of the licentiate iambic as he outlined it]; but he may alter it, *after the iudgment of his eare*, which Poets, Orators, and Musitions of all men ought to haue most excellent. *Quot homines, tot sententiae.*'

Campion designed the use of iambics, pure and licentiate, as 'those numbers which Nature in our English destinates to the Tragick and Heroick Poem: . . . in like manner being yet made a little more licentiate, that it may thereby the neerer imitate our common talke, will excellently serue for Comedies.'

The dimeter of the preceding discussion, *murmur at thy flight*, was Campion's second verse. It consisted of 'two feete and one odde sillable' which was common. Unfortunately, Campion allowed some combinations of dimeters in his illustrations, for example, the middle lines of the passage,

> *Rauing warre, begot*
> *In the thirstye sands*
> *Of the Lybian Iles*
> *Wasts our emptye fields*, etc.,

that were not so convincing as *murmur at thy flight* which was perfect in itself.

The third verse was the 'English Trochaick' regularly of five feet and especially suited to epigrams though 'it may be diuersely vsed.' The 'English Elegeick,' which was the fourth kind, was 'deriu'd out of our own naturall numbers as neere the imitation of the *Greekes* and *Latines* as our heauy sillables will permit.' The example quoted below is able to stand by itself as good blank verse. The first line is 'licentiate Iambick,' the second line, a combination of two dimeters.

> *Constant to none, but euer false to me,*
> *Traitor still to loue through thy faint desires,*
> *Not hope of pittee now nor vaine redresse*
> *Turns my griefs to teares, and renu'd laments*
> *Too well thy empty vowes, and hollow thoughts*
> *Witnes both thy wrongs and remorseles hart.* etc.

The next three numbers were lyrical forms, 'fit for *Ditties* or *Odes.*' It is among these that the famous unrimed poem, *Rose-cheekt Lawra*, occurs. The construction is a dimeter, two trochaical lines of four feet and one of two:

> *Rose-cheekt* Lawra, *come*
> *Sing thou smoothly with thy beawtie's*
> *Silent musick, either other*
> *Sweetely gracing.*
>
> *Louely formes do flowe*
> *From concent deuinely framed;*
> *Heau'n is musick, and thy beawtie's*
> *Birth is heauenly.*

> *These dull notes we sing*
> *Discords neede for helps to grace them,*
> *Only beawty purely louing*
> *Knowes no discord:*
>
> *But still moues delight,*
> *Like cleare springs renu'd by flowing,*
> *Euer perfet, euer in them-*
> *selues eternall.*

This poem, which has found its way into the *Oxford Book of English Verse*, justifies Campion's interest in the perfection of numbers free of rime. Its beauty lies in the subtlety of the rhythm and melody of the trochaic numbers of the poem as a whole as well as in such a detail of perfect sound as 'either other sweetly gracing.' Here the cadences 'close of themselues so perfectly that the help of rime were . . . superfluous.' Alliterative values heighten the effect while a more resonant beauty emanates from the vowel sounds. Assonance may further enrich the sound of these 'bare numbers' especially when the gradation is as beautiful as it is here. Echoes of various hues bind the stanzas together not only in the repetition of such words as *sing* and *beauty* but also in the ending *ly* of the words *smoothly, sweetly, lovely, purely,* and so forth.

The last number was called 'Anacreontick' verse 'to licentiate for a higher place, and in respect of the rest imperfect; yet is it passing gracefull in our English toong, and will excellently fit the subiect of a *Madrigall* [note the musical term], or any other lofty or tragicall matter.' For example,

Follow, followe,
Though with mischiefe
Arm'd, like whirlewind
Now she flyes thee;
Time can conquer
Loues vnkindnes;
Loue can alter
Times disgraces;
Till death faint not
Then but followe,

gains its effect through the use of the trochaic foot, assonance, and alliterative repetitions.

'These numbers,' Campion stated at the close of his exposition, 'which by my long obseruation I haue found
agreeable with the nature of our sillables, I haue set
forth for the benefit of our language, which I presume the
learned will not only imitate but also polish and amplifie
with their owne inuentions.'

But the importance of this treatise, in a discussion of
the relations of Elizabethan music and verse, is that during the course of his exposition, Campion coupled poetic
principles with musical analogies spontaneously. The fact
is that he appealed to music almost at once in his first
chapter. Through this appeal his attitude toward quantitative verse may be understood. He said that 'the world
is made by Simmetry and proportion, and is in that respect compared to Musick, and Musick to Poetry; for
Terence saith, speaking of Poets, *artem qui tractant musicam,*
confounding Musick and Poesy together. What Musick
can there be where there is no proportion obserued?'

Campion must have recognized that musical rhythms may be the same as verse rhythms (since the same was true of the ancients) when the length of notes or syllables govern the rhythm of either or both. Especially was this true for Elizabethan music where there was no definite accent and the rhythm was free. Campion's attention to the length of notes and syllables is disclosed in the following passage:

When we speake simply of number, we intend only the disseuer'd quantity; but when we speake of a Poeme, written in number, we consider not only the distinct number of the sillables, but also their value, which is contained in the length or shortnes of their sound. *As in Musick* we do not say a straine of so many notes, but so many sem'briefes . . . so in a verse the numeration of the sillables is not so much to be obserued as their waite and due proportion.

This statement shows that Campion clearly recognized quantity as the time- or sound-value of notes and syllables, and that he also recognized metrical equivalence. Since he thought not of strains of notes but of so many semi-breves, that is to say whole-notes, it may be deduced that a semi-breve is equal to a metrical foot. A semi-breve considered as a recognized unit of time in music, which may be broken up into any kind of smaller notes (minims equal to our half-notes, crotchets equal to quarter notes, quavers equal to eighth notes), is therefore synonymous with a metrical foot composed of the longs and shorts which are called iambic, trochaic, and so on, and metrical feet must be equal to each other. In thus treating metrical equivalence, Campion was also stating a quantitative aspect of musical and poetical sounds as the remainder of the quotation shows:

In ioyning of words to harmony there is nothing more offensiue to the eare then to place a long sillable with a short note, or a short sillable with a long note, though in the last the vowell often beares it out.

These statements of Campion closely resemble part of the context of an interesting passage that occurs in the Queens' College MS of Sidney's old *Arcadia* at the close of the first Eclogues.[1] Here the analogy of musical and poetical terms from the quantitative point of view is stated as follows:

Dicus said that since verses had their chief ornament in music, those that were justly appropriated to music agreed with music. Since music stood principally upon the sound and the quality, to answer the sound [the poets] brought words, to answer the quality they brought measure, so that every semi-breve or minim had its syllables matched accordingly with a long foot and a short foot, and without wresting the word, did kindly accompany the time, so that either by the time a poet should know how every word should be measured unto it, or by the verse as soon find out the full quantity of the music.

Campion, therefore, according to the common practice of the time, could not refrain from using the terminology of the two arts interchangeably. Today such practice would be considered extremely uncommon because of the widespread lack of knowledge of music. Yet the analogy still persists. That it is not generally recognized either by

1. This passage was first called to my attention by R.W.Zandvoort in his new study of the *Arcadia*, Amsterdam, 1929, pp.9-12. Its significance in relation to a discussion of Elizabethan music and verse is here used for the first time. I consider it unique testimony of the relationship.

literary experts or professors of poetry is only another illustration of the breach between poet and composer already discussed.

Is this passage, then, a source of Campion's work? Perhaps. Again, the perplexing characteristics of the age make any definite statement dangerous. The same ideas are certainly common to Sidney and Campion. But were they not common to the age? The brevity of Campion's *Observations* was to banish all possibility of obscurity. What was common knowledge in his time regarding musical and poetical analogies is confined to specialists today. Campion did not expect to be misunderstood, as his critics have misunderstood him, when he spoke of poetic principles in musical terms. Sound and proportion, derived from music, motivated his fashioning of an Art of Poetry. This quotation proves the source was music. It does not prove the source was Sidney.

Certainly Campion must have looked upon quantity in the broadest sense of the word as time- or sound-value. His position was similar to that of the American poet Sidney Lanier who stated that 'quantity is inseparable from all English words; though it is shifting, exactly as in music . . . And it is not limited in single proportions 1 to 2, but exists clearly in further proportions.'

The following musical setting may clarify this whole matter of Campion's approach to quantity.[2]

2. It does not follow, as Vivian points out in quoting the above passage on Campion's statement of quantity, that Campion 'naturally fitted the stronger accents to the longer notes.' (Cf.p.lx.) All the notes in the simple illustration which is given here do not bear this out. Nor is it exactly true that a strong accent involved a slightly increased time-period, thus misleading Campion. (Cf.p.lxii.) *Campion's Works*, P.Vivian, Oxford, 1909.

Shall I come, sweet Loue, to thee, when the eu' - ning beames are set? Shall I not ex - clud - ed be? Will you finde no fai - ned lett?

That most of the syllables in this example are considered of equal length is indicated by the quarter notes.
Campion uses half notes for *thee, set, be, lett*, in order to ob-
tain a variety of effects not quantitative but emphatic and
caesural. The eighth notes for *shall I* and *when thee* show
the elasticity of quantity where the meaning dictates
shortened sound. Increased excitement and buoyancy is
the result. An inconsistency appears in assigning the
preposition to a quarter note, but giving false quantities
to prepositions and conjunctions was a common fault of
Campion and other Elizabethans. It is often the result of
a too strict attention to classical rules of position which
the Elizabethan critics followed as far as reason would
allow. As a matter of fact, in singing the ayre, this dis-
crepancy would pass practically unnoticed because of the
length of the sound of *love*. This bears out a further ob-

servation in the Sidney MS to the effect that 'another time he would up in a long, that with being perchance but a light vowel, would be good with a breath [or rest].' In the final analysis, Campion would *leave it to the ear to judge*. It happens that in the third verse of the ayre the two notes given to *love to* in the first are taken by *danger*. These are subtle distinctions, but the ears of most musicians are sensitive organs and accustomed to nice discriminations.

The most confusing passage in the *Observations* occurs at the opening of Chapter IV:

I haue obserued, and so may any one that is either practis'd in singing, or hath a naturall eare able to time a song, that the Latine verses of sixe feete, as the *Heroick* and *Iambick*; or of fiue feete, as the *Trochaick*, are in nature all of the same length of sound with our English verses of fiue feete; for either of them being tim'd with the hand, *quinque perficiunt tempora*, they fill vp the quantity (as it were) of fiue sem' briefs; as for example, if any man will proue to time these verses with his hand.[3]

According to this passage, then, Campion would render *his* example of a Latin iambic line equal to the *sound* of five semi-breves, thus:

Suis   et   ipsa   Roma   viribus   ruit.

3. The beating of time was, as Vivian says (footnote, p.lxiv), such as that of a metronome. But Vivian errs in suggesting the beating of time by bars. Standard time on a metronome respects no barring with accents on first beats. And there were no bars *for this purpose* in Elizabethan music. To avoid all possible confusion only the pure iambic verse is considered in the following illustration.

A modern musican would indicate it:

With all disregard for discrepancies in the changing notation in music, the second version is the ideal transcription of the semi-breves above. At the same time, it expresses the true quantitative relationships based on time- or sound-values. A modern metrist might call this duple time (two beats to a measure or foot). There are five metrical divisions. The first and fourth are tribrachs or triplets but equal to the second, third, or fifth divisions.

The foregoing explanation may be clarified perhaps by forcing this line into a laboured triple measure for the sake of using the commonly recognized conventional barring in music where the musical accent is expected on the first beat of each measure. The line might then appear spaced in five equal measures as follows:

Su - is et   ip - sa Ro-ma   vir-i-bus ru - it.

The English example, if arranged in the last style, would run:

The more se - cure, the more the stroke we feele.

Campion says at this point that

The cause why these verses differing in feete yeeld the same length of sound, is by reason of some rests which either the necessity of the numbers, or the heauiness of the sillables do beget. For we find in musick that oftentimes the straines of a song cannot be reduct to true number without some rests prefixt in the beginning and middle, as also at the close if need requires. Besides, our English monosillables enforce many breathings which no doubt greatly lengthen a verse, so that it is no wonder if for these reasons our English verses of fiue feete hold pace with the *Latines* of sixe.

It is not stretching the point to show that this five-measure line may comply with the last clause of the quotation calling for six measures, as follows, though the illustration, forced as it is, is a distortion musically.

The more   se - cure, the more   the stroke   we feele.

The interpretation of this passage as a whole shows why Campion so quickly ruled out any thought of English hexameters. It further illustrates how closely music and poetry were associated in Campion's mind. That he had a definite idea of the *true* nature of quantity should now be clear.

An eighteenth-century writer on prosody, Joshua Steele, made a similar observation to the one just discussed above. He pointed out that

Poetry is often read [aloud] in a certain formal manner, supposing the ten syllables of *our heroics* must be cut exactly into five *cadences* of two syllables in each . . . whereas they always require the *time* of *six cadences* at least; but those who have only the idea of five *cadences*, seldom attend to the neces-

sary *rests* or *pauses*, or to a nice *metrical* sub-division of the
cadences according to the natural and necessary *emphasis* (or
poize) and *quantity* of each syllable; and therefore frequently
misplace the *light* and the *heavy*.

Another observation is made by Campion in this passage, which he does not illustrate: the matter of rests.
But the second sentence of the second part of the quotation links him with modern metrists. Lanier finds that
rests are 'quite as necessary to many forms of verse as
are the sounds thereof.' This may be seen in the nursery
rime :

> *Pease porridge hot*
> *Pease porridge cold*
> *Pease porridge in the pot*
> *Nine days old.*

The third line gives the time-value of four beats in full,
while the remaining lines are made complete by rests at
the end of each line filling out the sound-equivalence or
the line-rhythm. But the rest should not be confused with
a natural pause or caesura. Rests have quantitative values,
caesuras are rhetorical pauses. Gascoigne makes an interesting observation on this caesural pause. 'There are also
certayne pauses or restes in a verse, whiche may be called
Caesures, whereof I woulde be lothe to stande long, since
it is at discretion of the wryter, and they haue bene first
deuised (as should seeme) by the Musicians.'

Chapter X of the *Observations* considers the question of
determining quantity. Campion believed that quantity
was of prime importance but pointed out at the start that
the English might challenge much more licence than the

Greeks in determining it, 'by reason it stands chiefely
vpon monosillables, which, in expressing with the voyce,
are of a heauy cariage.' Quantity is accordingly determined as follows:

> But aboue all the accent of our words is diligently to be
> obseru'd, for chiefely by the accent in any language the true
> value of the sillables is to be measured. Neither can I remember
> any impediment except position that can alter the accent of
> any sillable in our English verse. For though we accent the
> second of *Trumpington* short, yet is it naturally long, and so of
> necessity must be held of euery composer.

This passage does not offer as much difficulty as it
might if a satisfactory definition of *accent* can be found.[4]
When Campion states that 'we accent the second of
Trumpington short, yet it is naturally long [by position],'
what does he mean? He does *not* use accent here in the
sense of metrical accent, or stress, but in the sense of
speech-accent or inflection, the alteration of pitch, or
more commonly, pronunciation. For instance, in the following observations on quantity, either the rising or
falling inflection determines the long syllable, while the
other syllables are short. The pronunciation is correct
even today.

> In words of two sillables, if the last haue a full and rising
> accent that sticks long vpon the voyce, the first sillable is
> alwayes short, vnlesse position, or the dipthong, doth make it
> long, as desire, preserve, define . . . Words of two sillables

4. The following interpretation is contrary to Vivian who believed Campion
   confused quantity and accent (Cf.pp.lxii–lxiii). The evidence, however, as
   we have seen in the preceding pages, points to Campion's full comprehension
   of quantity in its true sense because of his constant use of the terminology
   of both arts interchangeably.

that in their last sillable mayntayne a flat or falling accent, ought to hold their first sillable long, as rigor, glorie, spirit . . .[5]

Substitute pronunciation or speech-accent for 'accent' in the original quotation and it appears to be the solution *especially since Campion is discussing the quantity of words and not quantitative verse.*

The quantity of English syllables, therefore, is determined by natural pronunciation or speech-accent, and position. The key to all this is *sound*. 'Because our English Orthography . . . differs from our common pronunciation, *we must esteeme our sillables as we speake, not as we write, for the sound of them in a verse is to be valued and not their letters.*' This interpretation recognizes quantity as fundamental in English verse. 'English words, if pronounced accurately,' says W.J.Stone, 'have a distinct quantity, which is easily perceived by any one who will attend to it.' Quantity in its true sense is temporal. Campion probably recognized it in this sense because of his musical knowledge. In mentioning *Trumpington*, he was not confused. The second syllable, even though inflected short, can be long by position without changing the length of the first syllable as sound-value to any appreciable extent. In using the word, the following observation of T.S.Omond might be made: 'Stresses without time cannot make verse; when conditioned by time, they cease to be fundamental.'

But this question of quantity and metrical accent was a stumbling block for the earlier Elizabethans. They generally spoke of quantity to mean that of classical meters used in English. This came about through the movement started by Ascham's advocation of quantity in English poetry at the same time that he attacked the degradation of riming verse. Interest in the use of classical or quantitative meters was stimulated by the work of Sidney and Dyer and by the formation of the Areopagus which 'prescribed certaine Lawes and rules of Quantities of English sillables for English Verse' according to classical models. Also in circulation at this time were the rules of Master Drant which are not extant. Among the enthusiasts was Gabriel Harvey, who had evidently composed verse in this manner for some time, since he had occasion to express the hope that 'If I neuer deserue anye better remembraunce, let mee rather be epitaphed, the Inuentour of the English Hexameter.' To him came Edmund Spenser for advice.

Spenser found that in writing quantitative verse he had considerable difficulty with accent

whyche sometime gapeth, and, as it were, yawneth ilfauouredly, comming shorte of that it should, and sometime exceeding the measure of the Number, as in Carpenter the middle sillable, being vsed shorte in speache, when it shall be read long in Verse, seemeth like a lame Gosling that draweth one legge after hir . . . For why, a Gods name, may not we, as else the Greekes, haue the kingdome of oure owne Language, and measure our Accentes by the sounde, reseruing the Quantitie to the Verse?

Harvey replied thus:

you shal neuer haue my subscription or consent (though you should charge me wyth the authoritie of fiue hundredth

Maister DRANTS) to make your *Carpēnter*, our *Carpēnter*, an inche longer or bigger than God and his Englishe people haue made him . . . In shorte, this is the verie shorte and the long: Position neither maketh shorte nor long in oure Tongue, but so farre as we can get hir good leaue.

Both men have interpreted accent as metrical stress. The controversy over carpenter shows that the heart of the conflict was the attempt to reconcile the quantitative verse of the ancients with the accentual or stress verse of the moderns.

Sidney stated the situation succinctly:

The Auncient marked the quantitie of each silable, and according to that framed his verse; the Moderne obseruing onely number (with some regarde of the accent), the chiefe life of it standeth in that lyke sounding of the words, which wee call Ryme . . . The Auncient (no doubt) more fit for Musick, both words and tune obseruing quantity . . . The latter likewise, with hys Ryme, striketh a certaine musick to the eare . . . Truely the English, before any other vulgar language I know, is *fit for both sorts*.

But Sidney in illustrating quantitative verse forced his measures, while Campion, in following the principles outlined in his *Observations*, could write a single line.

And tell the rauisher of my soule I perish for her loue

so that 'it would quite spoil the music of the verse to read with strong [metrical] accents on the stressed syllables.' The difference between Sidney and Campion lies in the fact that Campion's ear told him of subtle varieties of quantitative values which Sidney never seems to have caught.

When Daniel wrote that 'you cannot make this fall into the right sound of verse,

Campion— "None thinkes reward rendred worthy his worth,"
Daniel—

vnlesse you thus misplace the accent vpon *Rendred* and *Worthie*, contrary to the nature of these wordes,' he was thinking in terms of accentual verse and appeared bound to a pure iambic line determined by stress. The line would, from this point of view, contain two false accents. Campion, however, would have accepted this line as quantitative verse (probably licentiate iambic) because his ear recognized no false accents as stresses. In addition, by thinking quantitatively, he would maintain with T.S.Omond that 'regularity of accentuation is no canon of English verse.'

In the final analysis, W.J.Stone declares that he would define the difference between ancient and modern meters thus:

in the one the verse scans by quantity alone, the accent being used only as an ornament, to avoid monotony: in the other the functions are exactly reversed, the accent deciding the scansion, the quantity giving variety. *The final result on the ear I believe to be very much the same,* but whereas we attend (theoretically) to accent exclusively and are only unconsciously affected by quantity, with the ancients the position was reversed.

This last statement was in all probability Campion's point of view, so sensitive was his musician's ear to the time-value of sounds. His verse may often be read accentually for it is not at all uncommon to find long syllables stressed. It is not, however, regular accentual verse but quantitative verse filled with an infinite variety of gradations of sound-values.

In the twentieth century as the tide turns back to numbers without rime, quantity, or time-value, is recognized as the foundation of verse. This recognition is based on scientific experiment. Experimentation shows that there can be no accent until there is a sound, and that as soon as there is sound, there is quantity. In determining quantity, however, as Campion says at the end of his *Observations*: 'as the Grammarians leaue many sillables to the authority of Poets, so do I likewise leaue many to their iudgments; and withall thus conclude, that there is no Art begun and perfected at one enterprise.'

VI

THE MUSICIAN AS POET

IN the earlier chapters, the attempt to show that music
and poetry marched hand in hand during the age of
Elizabeth and the early seventeenth century was necessarily confined to general observations. In fact, as the
evidence from the Sidney MS, to which reference was
made in the preceding chapter, shows, Elizabethan poets
constantly mixed the terminology of music with that of
poetry. Music was so prevalent that poets could hardly
escape its influence. Not only was it spoken of in poetical
terms, but poetry was measured by musical notes. Such a
confusion of terms suggests the establishment of a musical prosody for poetry since the poet knew by means of
the time the value of the words and by means of the verse
the quantity of the music. Considering the lyric, then,
in terms of its musical qualities or the possible musical
setting in store for it, it is evident that the Elizabethan
poets must have written verses for music as a matter of
course.

Campion, writing in retrospect, tells his reader in the
1619 book of Latin epigrams, that it was Apollo who not
only led him into the field of medicine, but also taught
him how to adapt words to music, and that he ever re-
joiced in yielding to Apollo's admonitions:

In medicos vbi me campos deduxit Apollo,
Aptare et doucuit verba Britanna sonis:
Namque in honore mihi semper fuit vnicus ille,
Cuius ego monitis obsequor vsque lubens.

The interrelationship of music and poetry was noted in the more familiar quotation which occurs toward the end of his address to the reader of his *Two Bookes of Ayres*, where he says: 'I haue chiefely aymed to couple my Words and Notes louingly together.' That intimacy between verse and music as found in Campion, the musical poet, is the subject of the following chapters.

By the time Campion emerged as a writer of ayres, however, music had already conditioned the Elizabethan lyric. Composers of madrigal music subject to the technical rules of that type of composition had made certain demands of poets aspiring to musical settings for their poems in matters of form, content, and style. First, the poem must be short and express a single mood. The common form of madrigal verse was composed of six lines. If there were several stanzas to a poem perhaps only one was set to the music, the remaining stanzas were either quoted with the music or else ignored, while a sonnet was generally considered to be the maximum length adapted to a single appropriate musical setting.

In addition to the matter of form, the emotional content of the poem was limited since it was usually conveyed by the music. The conventions of the times prohibited too great a display of emotion. Nor could a poem delve too far into the subtleties of thought. Words might

touch emotion, or suggest feeling, but they could not express weighty ideas, otherwise the entire aura of the
combination of music and words would be destroyed.

Simplicity was the key-note of the lyric style; simplicity attained through the use of concrete words, the avoid-
ance of abstractions, the sparing use of adjectives; simplicity attained through the use of conventional phrases
and clichés, and the device of repetition. For, as we have
seen, it is the rule in unaccompanied song that every
word must be heard.

Almost any poem of Campion immediately illustrates
these conditions. As an example, the lyric of the first
ayre in the 1601 *Booke of Ayres* will suffice. It happens to
be written in six-line stanzas. Though the first stanza is a
perfect translation of Catallus' 'Vivamus, mea Lesbia,
atque amemus,' the whole lyric contains only one emotional mood. The language is clear and open, not over-
charged with feeling, not too subtle, and thus complies
with the demands of the composers. The last line in each
stanza is a disguised refrain while the phrase 'euer-during
night' is suitable for repetition at the end of the melody.
The poem is quoted in full.

My sweetest Lesbia let vs liue and loue,
And though the sager sort our deeds reproue,
Let vs not way them: heau'ns great lampes doe diue
Into their west, and strait againe reuiue,
But soone as once set is our little light,
Then must we sleepe one euer-during night.

If all would lead their liues in loue like mee,
Then bloudie swords and armour should not be,

No drum nor trumpet peaceful sleepes should moue,
Vnles alar'me came from the campe of loue;
But fooles do liue, and wast their little light,
And seeke with paine their euer-during night.

When timely death my life and fortune ends,
Let not my hearse be vext with mourning friends,
But let all louers rich with triumph come,
And wish sweet pastimes grace my happie tomb;
And Lesbia close vp thou my little light,
And crowne with loue my euer-during night.

In naming the sonnet as the longest form susceptible of a musical setting, some consideration might be made in passing of the peculiar character of the Elizabethan form and how it was set to music. As we have seen, the Elizabethans used the words sonnet and song indiscriminately. It is well known that the Elizabethan sonnet as a poetical form differs from the Petrarchian in having three four-line groupings with a couplet to complete the required fourteen lines in contrast to the octave and sestet of the Italian form. It is not so well known, perhaps, that these quatrains suggest that many Elizabethan sonnets may be lyrics of three stanzas, with the addition of a couplet, combined in such a way that they may more readily serve as verses in a musical setting. This may be, in part, the explanation of the use of song and sonnet interchangeably. The demands of the composers for short stanzas and a single emotional mood make such an interpretation probable, while an interesting situation in connection with Campion is worth noting for the light that it may throw on this subject.

A certain manuscript of miscellaneous verse has been found containing three sonnets attributed to Campion that indicate some relationship to two of his ayres. Whether the stanzas of the ayres have been culled from the sonnets or the sonnets made by combining the stanzas of the ayres, is not quite certain since all evidence from dates is lacking. Of the two assumptions, however, the second appears to be the more logical. For example, the twelfth ayre in the 1601 *Booke of Ayres*, beginning 'Thou art faire for all thy red and white,' is divided into two stanzas of six lines each. The first stanza has been entirely absorbed in one of these sonnets by having the first four lines begin the sonnet while the remaining two make up the concluding couplet. The lines that come in between these merely expand the matter of the first four. Three lines of the second stanza of the ayre serve to end another sonnet on a similar idea.

The other case is of more significance. The ayre, 'Thrice tosse these Oaken ashes,' from the *Third Booke of Ayres*, is in three stanzas of four lines each. By inserting two lines in the combination of the three stanzas, the result obtained is the third sonnet of the manuscript just mentioned, which reads as follows:

> *Thrice tosse those oaken ashes in the ayer*
> *And thrice three tymes tye up this true lou's Knot;*
> *Thrice sitt you downe in this inchanted chaire*
> *And murmure softe Shee will or shee will not,*
> *Goe burne those poysoned weeds in that blew fyre,*
> *This Cypres gathered out a dead mans graue,*
> *These Scretchowles fethers and the prickling bryer*

That all thy Thornye cares an end may haue.
Then come you fairyes, daunce with mee a round,
Dance in a circle, let my loue be center.
Melodiously breathe an inchanted sound,
Melt her hard hart that some remorse may enter.
In vain are all the Charmes I can deuise;
She hath an arte to breake them with her eyes.

It happens that in this sonnet, lines 2 and 3 and lines 6 and 7 are reversed from the natural order in the musical setting in order that they may conform with the regular rime scheme of the sonnet form. The continuity of the thought is untouched by this alteration. Line 10 is an addition while lines 11 and 12 have been fashioned out of the expression confined to a single line in the ayre.

Thus these sonnets of Campion seem to have grown out of the ayres and probably reverse the normal procedure among Elizabethan poets and composers in general. The whole situation, however it may be interpreted, only emphasizes the conditioning of Elizabethan verse by the requirements necessary for a good musical setting. In either case, the form of the sonnet is Elizabethan.

One word more might be added on the manner in which music definitely dictates the form of Elizabethan verse. Wherever several stanzas are sung to the same melody, either the poet first composed his words to fit the notes of a melody already in existence so that the verses had to conform, or, when no melody was available, the poet kept strictly within the rhythmical and emotional limits of his first stanza if he wished his succeeding stanzas to fit the melody that might be written to the

first. Such practice would upon constant repetition condition the style of the lyrics themselves provided the
musical fashion of the period remained the same. As we
shall see in more detail in the close study of Campion's
ayres, the degree in which the words of successive stanzas
fit the music determines the artistry of the result. For this
is perhaps the most detailed way in which music can
definitely affect poetry.

The use of refrains and short word phrases in the lyrics
was essential to a madrigal composer because the elaborate polyphonic character of his music required repetitions. At the same time, it offered the poets a clever
device for pointing up a poem, and they readily grasped
this epigrammatic opportunity. In the third ayre of the
1601 collection, Campion uses a ten-line stanza of which
four lines are refrain. The effect of this refrain is to give
the lyric its essentially light-hearted character. It is
quoted in full.

> *I care not for these Ladies*
> *That must be woode and praide,*
> *Give me kind Amarillis*
> *The wanton country maide;*
> *Nature art disdaineth,*
> *Her beautie is her owne;*
>   *Her when we court and kisse,*
>   *She cries forsooth let go.*
>   *But when we come where comfort is*
>   *She neuer will say no.*
>
> *If I loue Amarillis,*
> *She giues me fruit and flowers,*

But if we loue these Ladies,
We must giue golden showers,
Giue them gold that sell loue,
Giue me the Nutbrowne lasse,
   Who when we court and kiss,
   She cries forsooth let go.
   But when we come where comfort is
   She neuer will say no.

These Ladies must haue pillowes,
And beds by strangers wrought,
Giue me a Bower of willowes,
Of mosse and leaues vnbought,
And fresh Amarillis,
With milke and honie fed,
   Who, when we court and kiss
   She cries forsooth let go.
   But when we come where comfort is
   She neuer will say no.

Again in 'My loue hath vowd hee will forsake mee' in the same collection, the last line of the first stanza, 'I will go no more a-maying,' is repeated at the end of the lyric to make a decided case in point. One of the most unusual uses of refrain occurs in still another ayre from the same book, 'Harke, al you ladies that do sleep,' in which the second line, 'The fayry queen Proserpina,' is repeated as a refrain in each of the five stanzas in the same position.

The repetition of a short word-phrase carried greater significance in the music than in the lyric, though in the hands of a clever poet it could be used to considerable advantage in the latter. Campion's ayres, we shall find, are studded with such repetitions and, in almost every case, they have been used with telling effect. This effectiveness, however, has been entirely lost in the reprints of the lyrics in literary form. To a scholar of the purely literary aspects of the Elizabethan song-books the matter of repetitions in the ayre has presented a delicate problem. The difficulty lay partly in his lack of understanding the nature of Elizabethan music and the musical aspects of the madrigal and the ayre; and partly in his adherence to the modern idea that repetitions not only do not belong in poetry but often weaken the effect while they appear frequently to strengthen effects in music. Repeated word phrases were primarily rhythmical devices in the madrigal where the polyphonic character of the music called for contrasts between the various voices, each singing independently of the other. A scholar specially interested in madrigal verse would generally omit these repetitions in reprints of the words in literary form. But in Campion's ayres, which were written for solo voice, there was no confusion of voices and nothing to obscure the meaning of the words. Consequently, repeated phrases in the music of the ayre carried far more weight in relation to the context of the words than in the madrigal. In the reprints of the words of the ayres, then, the omission of these repetitions involves a serious loss in the realization of the total effect of the ayre.

In spite of the idea that repetitions do not belong in poetry, repetitions often strengthen the emotional content of a lyric. In the case of Campion, they bring out all the subtle innuendoes that make the whole point of the meaning. This interdependence to be found between the words and music in the repetitions in his ayres proves the relationship of music and verse in a small way. The fact may be verified not only in the following illustrations, but also in many of the ayres to be considered in the next chapters.

The first example, from the *Third Booke of Ayres*, contains a short repetition, but at once a difference in effectiveness may be noted when the lyric and the ayre are set side by side.

Shall I come, sweet Loue, to thee, When the eu'-ning beames are set? Shall I not ex-clud-ed be? Will you finde no fai-ned lett? Let me not, for pit-ty,

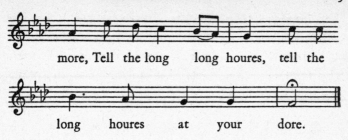

more, Tell the long   long houres, tell the

long   houres   at   your   dore.

Shall I come, sweet Loue, to thee,
When the eu'ning beames are set?
Shall I not excluded be?
Will you finde no fained lett?
Let me not, for pitty, more,
Tell the long houres at your dore.

In the printed lyric, the effect of the last line, 'Tell the
long houres at your dore,' is perhaps persuasive and informative, but in the ayre, the repetition of the line is not
only more informative, but far more expressive of the
weariness of waiting. All this is brought out in the music
by the descending line of melody and the lengthening of
the notes assigned to *long* which together convey the
feeling of weariness. While the lyric only suggests this
point, the ayre makes it effectively through the device of
repetition.

The second illustration, from the *Fourth Booke of Ayres*,
contains an extended repetition the effectiveness of which
will probably be self-evident.

In the reprint of the words of this ayre, the phrase 'but a little higher' is given only twice. The constant repetition of the words in the ayre itself, heightened each time by the fact that the musical arrangement of the phrase begins a whole tone above the preceding one with each repetition, makes the total effect somewhat startling. The musical setting of the phrase is ingenious for the down and upward curve of the melodic line.

seeke Loue's flame so low? But a lit-tle

higher, but a lit-tle higher, but a lit-tle

higher, but a lit-tle higher,

There, there, O there lives Cu-pids fire.

The point in many of Campion's lyrics is, therefore, somewhat obscured in the literary transcripts of the words through the omission of the repetitions which are as significant to the verse as they are to the music. The reason for this significance is, of course, the epigrammatic flavour of Campion's style. The musician as poet recognized how readily the meaning of the words carried over into the expression of the music. He also understood that where in many cases needless repetitions occur in songs, occasions do arise when they are emphatically useful. The complementary use of them in the words and music of the ayres is consequently important in the relationship of music to verse.

But the relation of the two was far closer than this discussion of the form, content, and style of the Elizabethan lyric suggests.

VII

THE MUSICAL POET

IN order to understand how it was possible for an Elizabethan musical poet to work in the two arts simultaneously, it will be necessary to consider the characteristics of the music of that period. For practically three centuries, erroneous ideas have been circulated concerning the nature of Elizabethan music, and for that matter, as we have seen, the Elizabethan lyric. Dr. Burney's pronouncement in the latter half of the eighteenth century that 'those who are not accustomed to the music of the sixteenth century, will be much embarrassed with the broken phrases and false accents of the melody, in which there is so total a want of rhythm, as renders the time extremely difficult to keep with accuracy and firmness,' expresses a point of view held for almost a century before and over a century after his time. He further maintained that 'taste, rhythm, accent, and grace, must not be sought for in this [Elizabethan] kind of music; indeed we might as well censure the ancient Greeks for not writing in English, as the composers of the sixteenth century for their deficiency in these particulars, which having then no existence, even in idea, could not be wanted or expected.'

Yet just the opposite was true. The situation was similar to Dryden's misreading of Chaucer because he did not grasp the medium in which Chaucer wrote. Brought

up on music which dated from the middle of the seventeenth century as the *only* kind of music, Dr. Burney
could hardly have understood that the phrases of Elizabethan music were not broken, the accents not false, the
rhythm not wanting, the time probably more strictly
observed than in the music of the modern age, the grace
and charm of the music far more spontaneous. Today
there is no feeling of embarrassment on hearing this music of the Elizabethans, but rather a feeling of relief from
the regular conventions of eighteenth-century practice.

The story of the difference between modern and Elizabethan music may be told briefly by looking at any
printed page of music. The appearance of the five-line
staff, the use of treble and bass clefs, the key signatures
in sharps or flats, the time signatures of three-four, four-
four, six-eight, and so forth, the line of music divided
into equal spaces of time called measures, and designated
by bars: all this is familiar. But a page of music written
for Queen Elizabeth's virginal, which at first glance
might appear similar to a page of modern music, on closer
inspection would prove quite different. The staff would
be of six lines; the clef signs might or might not be familiar; there would be no key signatures in the modern
sense; the bar lines would not mean equal measures of
time. Only the notes would approach values approximately the same, and even they have become more
rounded in shape in modern musical notation.

In secular song, to which the ayres belong, the five-line
staff had been common since about 1500. An ayre with a
lute accompaniment would therefore have a five-line staff
for the voice melody and a six-line staff for the accom-

paniment. This arrangement may be seen in any reproductions of the original ayres (Frontispiece and Plate I). They should be compared with a modern transcription (Plate II), to illustrate all the differences outlined above. Only the details of such differences as bear on the subject of this chapter will be considered.

The story may also be told in another way. Music is generally considered to be fashioned out of the three elements: rhythm, melody, and harmony. Elizabethan music was primarily rhythmic and melodic, and harmony existed only by accident or courtesy. Music since the middle of the seventeenth century has become more and more indebted to harmony with increasingly less attention paid to melody and rhythm *per se*. Rhythm has suffered the most, for the general conception of rhythm today is not rhythmical but metrical. It is based on the square-cut design of measures of equal time units generally lasting throughout an entire composition—on 'four-measure phrases,' two of which make an 'eight-measure period,' two of which make a 'sixteen-measure or double period' and so on, in the name of symmetry. All this is not unlike the format of a poem in the heroic couplet in the late seventeenth- and eighteenth-century literature, the establishment of which took place at relatively the same period as that of 'measured music.' The dictator of this so-called measured music was the bar line. Its sceptred sway has only been questioned within the last half-century.

For three centuries, rhythm has been threatened with confinement within definite limits, of measures in the case of music, of feet in the case of poetry, by the bar line.

It has not only marked off equal divisions of time, indicated by time signatures at the beginning of musical compositions to record the number of beats in a measure, and by such labels as 'iambic pentameter' or 'trochaic trimeter' in poetry to record the number of feet in a line, but in music it has established an unwritten but nevertheless regular accent on the first or strong beat of every measure. Since English metrists have persistently shunned the metrical analogy of poetry and music, the accent in poetry has no definite relation to the bar line or foot division, though it well might have because, in the case of both music and poetry, attention to accent has chained down rhythm to a metrical basis. The effect of the bar line in modern settings of songs may be seen in the well-known anthem, 'My Country 'tis of Thee,' which is usually written in three-four time. Daniel Gregory Mason has pointed out that were the time signature three-two, the anthem would gain immeasurably in dignity and repose, as the following illustration shows, because of the change in metrical grouping.

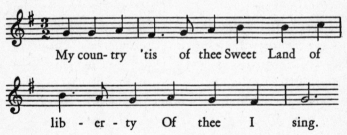

My coun- try 'tis of thee Sweet Land of lib - er - ty Of thee I sing.

Neither version, unfortunately, avoids the superfluous strong accent on 'tis; but while the 3/4 makes us say 'My country, 'tis of thee, Sweet land of liberty, Of thee I *sing*'—which is about as wrong as it could be—the 3/2 . . . gives us the obviously far more just: 'My *country* '*tis* of *thee*, Sweet *land* of *lib*erty, Of *thee* I *sing*.'

This new version suggests that the three lines of verse might be considered as a single phrase with the flow of rhythm sweeping through from the beginning to a rhythmical accent on *sing*. Such an interpretation would then ignore even further the restrictions of the bar line which characterize the generally accepted version. That such imprisonment was not the case with music in the Elizabethan period may at once be noted in the melody on page 121 reproduced from the original of the first ayre in Campion's *Fourth Booke of Ayres*.

Here the bar lines neither indicate equal divisions of time by beats nor suggest metrical accents for the first note of every measure, but serve as a convenience for the eye to keep the melody and accompaniment together. In contrast to the modern significance of the bar line as a metrical device, then, the Elizabethan use of it is merely graphic. The time signatures appearing in this example do not indicate the number of beats to the measure, but are part of the medieval conception of *tempus perfectum* or *tempus imperfectum*, which is quite outside of consideration here. If any confusion should exist from this explanation of the insignificance of bar lines in this music as opposed to the high significance in modern music, the slurs over the bar line showing that the two notes at the same pitch for *leaue* or *mourning* are one sound, eliminates further doubt. No bar lines whatsoever appeared in the separate voice parts of madrigals or in the suggested bass solos sometimes written for the ayres (cf. frontispiece).

Leaue pro - long - ing, leaue pro-

long - ing, thy dis - tresse, All de-

layes af - flict the dy - ing.

Ma - ny lost sighes long I

spent, to her for mer - cy cry - ing;

But now vaine mourn - ing cease, Ile dye, Ile

dye, and mine owne griefes re - lease.

This whole discussion, then, points to this conclusion; namely, that there was no regularly recurring metrical accent in Elizabethan music, except, of course, in the dance, as we conceive such an accent in modern music. Indeed, there could be no sense of musical accent. The flow of time in their music was considered as constant as the monotonous beat indicated by a metronome since it was indicated by the kind of note: semi-breves, minims, and the like equivalents. Each note held an exact mathematical proportion to every other note. 'Time' was quantity or the due proportion of sounds. In other words, a long syllable demanded not a stronger accent but a greater length of time. Shakespeare recognizes this phenomenon in Act V, SCENE v, of *Richard II*:

> *Music do I hear?*
> *Ha Ha! keep time;—how sour sweet music is*
> *When time is broke and no proportion kept!*

The Sidney manuscript says: 'So that eyther by the time a poet should knowe how euery worde should be measured unto yt, or by the verse assone finde out the full quantitie of ye musicke.' Campion says: 'In ioyning of words to harmony there is nothing more offensiue to the eare then to place a long sillable with a short note or a short sillable with a long note, though in the last the vowell often beares it out.' Poets and musicians, in the observance of time or proportion of sounds, thus met on common ground. Indeed, the Elizabethans in order to sing their madrigals generally had to have a keen sense of time.

But there is another conclusion to this discussion. The absence of accent in Elizabethan music is negative evidence. What the observance of strict time brings, is rhythm, free from all fetters. And rhythm was the *life* of Elizabethan music.

The other element of this music was melody which also manifested a freedom and subtlety that would seem alien to eighteenth-century conceptions of four-square melodies or melodies phrased in four measures. The 'broken measures' of which Dr. Burney speaks were melodies either stretched out into long lines or chopped into short phrases. Any attempt to impose a regular method of phrasing on such melodies naturally caused embarrassment since the phrasing is obviously irregular. The melody used above might be written thus:

Leaue pro - long-ing

leaue pro - long - ing thy dis - tresse,

All de - lays af - flict the dy - ing.

Many lost sighes long I spent, to her for mer - cy cry-ing:

But now vaine mourn - ing cease,

Ile dye

Ile dye, and mine owne griefes re - lease.

Melody, though it possesses distinct qualities of its own in giving a contour to a definite set of sounds, is, nevertheless, closely linked to rhythm. With the combination of the two, a certain quality enters called mood. A musical mood is emotion crystallized in sound. A melodic succession of sounds conforming to a rhythmic pattern might thus express an emotion. And in the Elizabethan age the emotion behind a lyric was generally found in the musical setting. The prevailing mood was one of lightness even when the cause might be meditative or sad, for a spirit more characteristic of the Cavalier than the Puritan was abroad in this age and the music had an inherent freshness and spontaneity of its own.

So Elizabethan music has these three characteristics: rhythm, melody, and mood. And the qualities of each are different from those of the later music because of a sense of freedom foreign to the modern age. Now the same thing might be said of Campion's lyric poetry. If by some commentators he is called a 'curious metrist' because of the infinite variety of metrical schemes in his verse, the reason may be found in his sense of rhythm. His lyrics are often said to sing themselves because of their melody. Furthermore, he knew how to capture a mood and seal it within the compass of an ayre so that it remained perennially fresh. Since Campion's ayres are the creation of a musical poet, some kind of union must be accounted for between the music and the poetry. This will be discovered in the close relations of the two in rhythm, melody, and mood.

Rhythm in music, poetry, and art in general is probably best defined as a certain order and proportion in space and time. Poets and musicians may think of it as a sense of motion leading toward a climax or an accent which is dictated by the sense of the words or the flow of a melody. In either case, it is a natural pulsation in a steady streaming motion. Meter is different. It signifies measure and a regularly recurring beat. When Dr. Burney said that Elizabethan music lacked rhythm, he meant meter because he found that the free flow of sounds in this earlier music did not conform to the metrical schemes in practice during the eighteenth century. His experience, however, reveals the general characteristic of rhythm; namely, that it transcends meter. In music, the rhythm of a whole composition must be considered greater than that of the phrases leading up to the finale, a melodic phrase greater than its measures; while in poetry, a stanza is greater than a group of lines, a line greater than the feet of which it is composed. The reason for this is that rhythm exists in nature while meter is a convention for measuring time.

This phenomenon is explained by Paul Elmer More in the following manner:

Listen to a good reader attentively, and for a while you will be able to beat time to the rhythm of the verse as accurately as to music; then suddenly, through some stress of feeling or some desire to avoid monotony, the rhythm will be loosened to an unmeasured flow of sounds, only to fall again into a regular singsong.

Such a thing happens in this modern age. It could hardly have happened in Elizabethan times because they recognized the true freedom of rhythm 'loosened to an un-

measured flow of sounds.' It cannot be over-emphasized
that rhythm was the life of this music. In the madrigals
it was constantly changing. Scarcely a madrigal exists in
which the rhythm is not frequently changed in all the
voice parts. In the melody 'Leaue prolonging' quoted
above, the first phrase is in a different rhythm from the
one following. To the singers these changes offered no
difficulty for it was as natural to them to sing a variety
of rhythms in succession as it would seem awkward to
us to shift from three-four to two-four to three-two time
within a few measures.

In an age where imagination knew no bounds and music was so well understood, it was only natural that the
poets should profit by this display of rhythmic freedom.
Shakespeare in writing his songs recognized it when he
was adapting an old ballad, as in the case of the Willow
Song in Act IV, SCENE III of *Othello,* or creating a new
song, as 'It was a lover and his lass' in Act, V, SCENE III
of *As You Like It*. But the meter of Shakespeare's blank
verse does not confine the rhythmic phrasing. For instance, the following speech of Horatio in Act I, SCENE I
of *Hamlet* is an interesting case:

> Hor. *So have I heard, and do in part believe it.*
> *But look, the morn, in russet mantle clad,*
> *Walks o'er the dew of yon high eastern hill:*
> *Break we our watch up: and, by my advice,*
> *Let us impart what we have seen tonight*
> *Unto young Hamlet.*

Break this metrical setting into its rhythmic phrases and
the result is:

So have I heard,
And do in part believe it.
But look,
The morn, in russet mantle clad, walks o'er the dew of yon high
eastern hill:
Break we our watch up,
And, by my advice,
Let us impart what we have seen tonight unto young Hamlet.[1]

That this breaking up of the metrical form into the rhythmical phrases can be done with any good blank verse of the Elizabethan period, is a phenomenon entirely in keeping with the freedom of music at this time. Blank verse flourished at a time when rhythm was unfettered. As soon as meter was emphasized, the heroic couplet predominated in poetry. In passing, it might be well to ask if Shakespeare's run-on lines may not claim some relationship to the free rhythms of Elizabethan music.

Turn to Campion with this interpretation of rhythm in mind, and his irregularities and varieties of 'meter' explain themselves. The previous example, 'Leaue prolonging,' illustrated this. The following ayre from the 1601 *Booke of Ayres* with its lines of varied length, does the same. The arrangement is taken from the musical phras-

1. This passage is cited by Sidney Lanier in his *Science of English Verse*, p.81. Lanier could not have made the present deduction because the true nature of Elizabethan music was unknown at that time. Lanier's conception of it must have been somewhat similar to that of Dr. Burney. He attributed the freedom illustrated in writing out the passage in rhythmical phrases to the nature of the poetry. Had he known the music as it is known today, there is room for little doubt that he would have elaborated this relationship and drawn the analogy.

ing since musical rhythm and verse rhythm are always in agreement.

Turne backe, you wanton flyer,
And answere my desire with mutuall greeting.
Yet bende a little nearer,
True beauty still shines cleerer in closer meeting.
Harts with harts delighted should striue to be vnited,
Either others armes with armes enchayning;
Harts with a thought, rosy lips with a kiss still entertaining.

But mention was made of rhythm as motion toward an accent. Since in Elizabethan music there was no metrical accent,—that is to say the rhythm was free—the only accent possible would be one based on literary sense. *This accent could be nothing but a rhythmical accent.* The natural stress, that is the pronunciation, of words in a phrase is, of course, present to some extent. But these stresses act only as an anacrusis toward this rhythmical accent based on meaning. In the line,

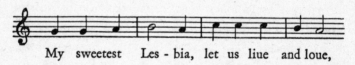

My   sweetest   Les - bia, let us liue   and loue,

the sweep of the rhythm carries through to the word *loue*. The line might be broken into two shorter phrases at the comma, but the real rhythmical accent or point of repose is on *loue* and to this the whole flow of the line is directed.

An interesting situation is presented in the ayre, 'I care not for these Ladies,' already quoted. It is a light ayre calling for a rapid tempo. At first glance it would seem that such a regular short-long scansion of iambic accents would produce a singsong effect, and that this example is not unlike the results obtained by observing modern metrical schemes. That such a thing should occur in Campion is not so strange since in a period of transition, suggestions of future form are often found in transitional writers. But this does not happen exactly, because the notes assigned to *Ladies* are of a longer value than any of the other notes. With their close attention to time, the Elizabethans would have found no accent elsewhere. This is what is meant by motion toward an accent when defining rhythm.

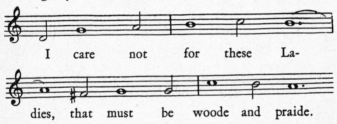

The fourth ayre in the *Fourth Booke of Ayres* shows how relatively unimportant word stress was to the Elizabethans. In the fourth line of both stanzas a word stress occurs written with a short note while the unstressed syllable has a long note.

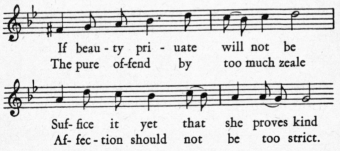

Both the words *suffice* and *affection* in the above illustration have quarter-notes for the unstressed and eighth-notes for the stressed syllables. In passing, however, note the effectiveness gained through the use of a quarter-note for *if* in the first verse while *the* becomes over-emphasized as a result of this in the second. *Too* in the second verse also receives emphasis by having the value of a quarter-note (two eighths) lengthen the duration of the word where an ordinary accentual reading would throw the emphasis on *much*.

But the next ayre, from the 1601 collection, should settle the matter of metrical accent.

> *Followe thy faire sunne, vnhappy shadowe,*
> *Though thou be blacke as night,*
> *And she made all of light,*
> *Yet follow thy faire sun, vnhappie shadowe.*

If the first line could be scanned as trochaic pentameter, the second and third lines iambic trimeter, the last line would make a metrist pause for an explanation. But metrists, interested primarily in scansion *per se* and the exact laws of metrical correspondence, must not be confused with rhythmists interested not in verse forms but forms of verse. The one conceives of verse from the rigidly proportional point of view, the other, from the artistic. Rhythmists do not deny proportion but they realize the possibilities of the variation within its limits that make for artistic effectiveness. Campion has been called a curious metrist by those who have scrutinized his verse forms and remained puzzled by such irregularities as those in the above stanza. Campion, however, was not a metrist at all, but a rhythmist, which, to put it harshly, is the difference between a mechanic and an artist. *The musical setting of the stanza shows that it is not 'scanned' as accentual verse as suggested above, but is composed quantitatively and rhythmically.* This seems to be proof of the quantitative position found in the Sidney manuscript quoted in the preceding chapter and Campion's position in his *Observations*.

But the musical setting proves more than this. It provides the basis of a musical prosody. Since words and notes are coupled lovingly together, any question of scansion is immediately settled by looking at the setting of the ayre, which in this case is as follows:

This particular ayre seems more 'measured' than many because the time pattern is regular and the measures are barred regularly. It might, therefore, be taken as an example of the transition to the form in modern music where the bar line has an accentual significance. At this period, however, the bar line was still graphic and the phrasing of the music quite irregular. The first phrase is of three measures, the second of two, and so on. The treatment of *shadow* in the first phrase is interesting. Recalling Campion's adherence to metrical equivalence and and rests in his *Observations*, which was discussed in the latter part of Chapter V, the reader will notice that the short time-values given to *shadow* are made up in the rest which follows the word. The whole measure is thus an equal unit of time with the others.

The free rhythm and irregular phrasing of the music may, therefore, be found to explain the 'metrical' variety in Campion's lyrics when they are separated from the musical settings. The difficulty of reading strong accents on the proper syllables in such a line as the one cited in Chapter V, 'And tell the rauisher of my soule I perish for her loue,' may now be more readily perceived. A metrical reading would spoil the artistic effect since the rhythm flowing through to the end of the line transcends all its parts. The source of this rhythmic freedom was, of course, the nature of Elizabethan music.

Thus in the ayres where the words and music are one, the first real meaning of their close relationship is discerned. But the observation of the rhythmic swing of an ayre immediately calls attention to the curve of its melody. So closely connected are these that it is almost impossible to discuss rhythmic schemes without considering melodic phrasing.

The twentieth century thinks harmonically whereas the sixteenth century thought melodically because the whole basis of musical expression in Tudor England was vocal. It would be natural to suppose, then, that in a people keenly alive to sound, the alliance between melody and speech would be closer than under different circumstances. That was true. The Elizabethan lyric is said to sing itself, a fact which may be interpreted to mean that the suggestion of a tune in the words of a lyric may be the musical overtones in the language itself. Sidney Lanier sensed this phenomenon when he wrote:

If having uttered the sentences in a rigidly unvarying tone, the reader will then utter them in the tunes which we feel— by some inward perceptions too subtle for treatment here— to be appropriate to them, it will be easily seen that the definite successions of tones are being used.

In other words, the melody of these Elizabethan lyrics may be a projection of the inflections of the words. Melody, then, brings words and music closer together so that the one will seem to suggest the other.

A study of the melodies of Campion's ayres reveal the musical poet at work, because music gives an eloquence to the words that enriches what the words have to say. The words uttered in speech should fall into certain contours which melody can heighten only through pitch. The skill with which the words and notes follow these contours will indicate the artistry of the composer.

An ayre already mentioned may serve to introduce the growth of the melodic significance in words. It is 'I care

not for these Ladies' in the 1601 collection. The first
phrase falls into a natural rhythm which the values of
the notes indicated. It also falls into a natural melody
illustrating the method which Lanier suggested. Though
in individual experiments in either speaking this line or
reading it out loud expressively, the inflections of the
voice might be somewhat different, the melodic curve of
the sounds produced would be about the same. Campion
hit on this happy melody for the line which serves
equally well for the next.

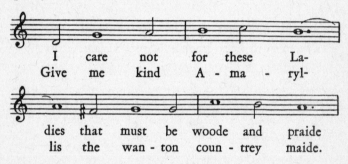

Rhythmically, such words as *care* and *must* in the first line
and *me* and *wan*ton in the second are interestingly emphasized by having a longer time-value assigned to them.
Melodically, the upward sweep of the first part of the
phrase follows the rising inflection of the recited line
while the latter part is distinguished by the emphasis on
woode and *coun*trey which would come from a natural inflection of the voice at this point because of the meaning
of the words. In passing, note that the same phrase is
used for different words but only because these different
words have the same inflection melodically and rhythmically.

Two clever touches come later in this ayre which are especially successful in showing the details of melodic treatment. The first records the inflectional stress according to the sense of the words:

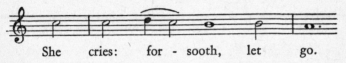

She   cries: for - sooth,   let   go.

Recalling the context of the lyric quoted in the preceding chapter, the reader will perceive that when 'she' anxiously cries 'forsooth,' her voice naturally records a higher note for the first syllable, even suggests the interesting two-note sound that Campion has given to it, and drops with the utterance of the succeeding words.

The second example speaks for itself by recording in the rise to the high note on *neuer* an emphasis which overrides the assignment of a long note to *will*, all of which perfectly outlines the inflection of the voice in saying 'she NEUER *will* say no.'

She   ne - uer   will   say   no.

From these examples, and many that follow, it may be seen how the melody underlines the inflection of the spoken line and even records the meaning behind the words implied in the context of the lyric. Naturally, therefore, the Elizabethan lyric may be said to sing itself if the melodies of the ayres record at least in part the inflections of the spoken poetry. The reason for this is, of course, simply that both music and poetry in this period were vocal and that music was a dominating force in Elizabethan life.

The melodic phrase may not only underline the inflections of the words, it may even depict a direct meaning of the words pictorially. The following two illustrations happen to allow both interpretations at the same time. The first,

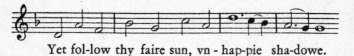

Yet fol-low thy faire sun, vn - hap-pie sha-dowe.

suggests following an upward path toward the light of the sun by means of the ascending nature of the melody in small step-up phrases culminating in the highest notes on *vnhappie* because of the emphatic inflection on this word. Thus the pictorial phrasing of the notes and the expression of the spoken words are combined effectively. In the second stanza, the words to the same music, 'yet follow her whose light the world reuiueth,' fit in the same ways since the meaning is similar. It happens that this melody is also used for the ayre 'Seeke the Lord' in the first of the *Two Bookes of Ayres*. That the handling of the melodic phrase is exactly the same in both the pictorial phrasing and the inflectional curve is a tribute to Campion's skill.

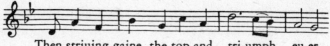

Then striuing gaine the top and tri-umph eu-er.

The second is a perfect example of the close union of words and notes. It not only agrees with the above explanation of pictorial phrasing, but also recalls the first characteristic of following the speech utterance of the words.

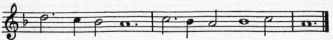

Fol - low your saint, fol-low with ac-cents sweet
Haste you sad notes, fall at her fly-ing feete.

The emphasis of the sense of the first phrase comes on *follow*, in the first line, and *haste* in the second. But in this case the pictorial curve of the notes is downward while in the preceding illustration it was upward. The reason is to be found in the connotation of the words *sad* and *fall* in the second line. The melodic curve of the second phrase differs from the first probably because of the change in inflection of the word *flying*.

In the ayre 'Awake, awake, thou heauy spright' in the first *Two Bookes of Ayres*, there are some more couplings of words and notes that are impressive. For instance the first phrase in both verses:

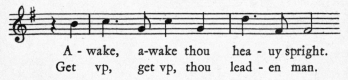

A - wake, a-wake thou hea - uy spright.
Get vp, get vp, thou lead - en man.

How naturally the sense is conveyed in the musical notation for *awake* and *get vp*, especially in the emphasis carried out by the larger interval between the notes in the repetition of the words. Again, different words are set to the same musical phrase, but how similar is the meaning and the effect in balancing *leaden* with *heauy*.

In the second example, from the same ayre,

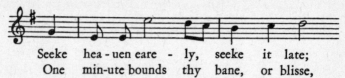

Seeke   hea - uen eare - ly,   seeke   it   late;
One   min-ute bounds   thy   bane,   or blisse,

the pictorial effect is realized in the large interval
through which the music literally bounds to illustrate
the meaning. But the fitting of words and notes in this
case is obviously not so perfect.

Campion is not always successful in his settings. He
has degrees of faultiness in details. The balance of the
rhythm in 'Kinde are her answeres' in the *Third Booke of
Ayres* is sufficient to cover up some awkwardness of word
and note in the first stanza while the second stanza is far
more happily wedded to the situation which is both
rhythmic and melodic. In the first stanza given below the
repeated melodic phrase is again present and, as before,
the words *breaks time* fit perfectly the first phrase *Kinde are
her answeres*. The effectiveness lies, of course, in the emphasis on *kinde* both melodically and rhythmically. But
the melodic phrases of the rest of the ayre are not distinguished and the pictorial phrasing of the line 'and
smooth words wing my hopes in vaine' is somewhat
overdone. The ayre is, nevertheless, of striking character.

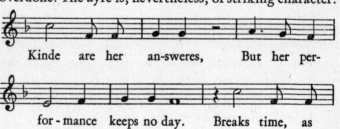

Kinde   are her   an-sweres,   But her per-
for - mance   keeps no day.   Breaks time,   as

dan - cers   From their own Mus - icke

when they stray.   All her free   fa - uors And

smooth words Wing my hopes   in vaine.

O   did eu - er   voice   so sweet but

on - ly fain?   Can true   loue yeeld such de-

lay,   con - uer - ting ioy   to   pain?

With the ayre 'When to her lute Corrina sings,' of the
1601 collection, the true master of melody and rhythm
appears. This is apparent in considering the ayre not
only as a complete unit but also in all its details. Sufficient explanation of preceding examples makes it unnecessary to point out the inflectional characteristics of the

melody, but certain instances of pictorial phrasing merit elucidation. In the second line, 'her voice reuiues the leaden stringes,' the idea of reviving is meant to be suggested in the diminutive curve of the notes written over the word. But the matter of the sighs recalls Thomas Morley's advice on how to treat them musically:

You may vse the crotchet or minime rest at the most, but a longer than a minime rest you may not vse, because it will rather seeme a breth taking then a sigh.

Campion has followed these instructions implicitly. The sigh is, of course, expressed in the rests between the notes. The fact that the phrases ascend is of no import since this is not the only way of writing them, though it is justified here from both an inflectional and expressive point of view.

When   to   her   lute   Cor - ri - na   sings,

Her voice   re - uiues   the   lead - en stringes,

And doth   in high - est   noates   ap - peare,

As   a - ny chal - leng'd   ec - cho cleere.

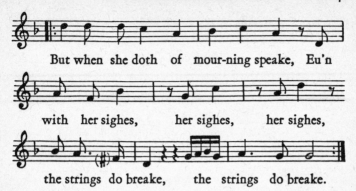

But when she doth of mour-ning speake, Eu'n

with her sighes, her sighes, her sighes,

the strings do breake, the strings do breake.

In matching the other verses, Campion was naturally confronted with the necessity of fitting important or contrasted words in the same positions in each stanza. He was most fortunate here, for instance, in matching such a phrase as 'And doth in highest noates appeare' with 'For when of pleasure she doth sing.'

Thus in the union of music and poetry in melody, two characteristics are disclosed: first, the successful transcription of spoken words into tone lines; and secondly, the pictorial treatment of phrases to outline direct or subtle meanings of the words. However, since rhythm is the life of melody, the tones of which may spring from some inward and emotional perception, it is no longer possible to conceal the state in which the two arts are definitely fused.

That state in which the union of music and poetry is consummated is the mood projected by the composer. This is the true meaning of Campion's statement in the preface to *Two Bookes of Ayres*: 'I haue aymed chiefely to couple my Words and Notes louingly together, *which will be much for him to doe that hath not power ouer both.*' His

additional remarks that 'the light of this will best appeare to him who hath paysd [weighed] our Monosyllables and Syllables combined, both of which, are so
loaded with Consonants, as that they will hardly keepe
company with swift Notes or giue the Vowell conuenient
liberty' are only the outward expression of his craftsmanship. The inward perception of wedding words and notes
is of equal if not greater importance. This inner expression is mood. The peerless settings of Shakespeare's 'Who
is Silvia?' and 'Hark, hark, the lark' came from a mood
in which the music and verse were perfectly wedded in
Schubert's mind. He was 'possessed' with his mood because he was saturated with the lyrical impulse underlying Shakespeare's words. Two strong imaginations fused
into one created those immortal songs.

The greatest of English composers, William Byrd, a
contemporary of Campion, testifies to the same feeling
that Schubert experienced. Byrd found that underlying
the words of his text were meanings that during serious
meditation seemed to clothe themselves in the right notes
in a strange way.

Porro, illis ipsis sententija (ut experiendo didici) adeo abstrusa
atq; recondita vis inest; vt diuina cogitanti, diligenterq; ac
serio peruolutanti; nescio quoniam modo, aptissimi quiq; nu-
meri, quasi sponte accurant sua; animoq; minime ignauo,
atq; inerti, liberaliter ipsi sese offerant.

In a similar mood, Campion must have conceived his
ayres. He had power over both arts, though he says himself in his Latin verse that music first taught him the way
to join words and notes together. *According to his own testimony, then, it must follow that words and music were usually*

composed spontaneously and simultaneously. The intricacies
of his rhythms and the adding of verses to the same melodies both testify to this creative method. His success
was hailed in a sonnet by a contemporary, John Davies
of Hereford, whose tribute appears highly justified:

> *Upon my selfe I should iust vengeance take,*
> *Should I omitt thy mention in my rime,*
> *Whose Lines and Notes do lullaby (awake)*
> *In heau'ns of pleasure, these unpleasant times.*
> *Never did Lyricks more then happie straines*
> *(Strained out of Arte by Nature, so, with ease,)*
> *So purely hitt the moods and various vaines*
> *Of musick and her hearers, as do these,*
> *So canst cure the body and the minde*
> *(Rare doctor) with thy two-fold soundest arte:*
> *Hippocrates hath taught thee the one kinde;*
> *Apollo and the Muse the other part:*
>   *And both so well, that thou with both dost please:*
>   *The minde with pleasure, and the corps with ease.*

Mood is the projection of whatever a composer feels.
Generally the Elizabethans expressed a spontaneous enthusiasm that never clouded too darkly their natural and
sincere light-heartedness. If Campion's lyrics, judged
without their musical settings seem lacking in warmth
or are said to be platonically cold, then, as a general rule,
the music adds the missing quality.

The mood of indifference is adroitly expressed in the
ayre 'I care not for these Ladies.' The first three words, 'I
care not' strike the mood and the whole ayre is framed in
an epigrammatic setting. It belongs to a whole group of

spirited ayres of various hues. Among these might be mentioned: 'Mistris, since you so much desire,' in the same 1601 collection; the rustic ditty 'Iacke and Ione' suggestive of a folk-song rhythm and melody, and such trifles as 'Young and simple though I am' in the later collections.

It is the mood that makes 'When thou must home to shades vnderground' in which neither rhythm nor melody is distinctive. In this case, the inflection of the words evokes a line of melody which conveys a mood of dignity. There are no pictorial phrasings, no rhythmically emphatic places, but just a meditative movement which casts its own spell through music written in what today is called the minor mode.

When thou must home to shades of   vn - der - ground,
The beau-teous spi-rits do   in-girt thee round

And there a - riu'd, a   newe ad - mir - ed guest,
White I - o - pe, blith Hel-len, and the   rest,

To   heare   the   sto - ries   of   thy

fin - isht   loue,   From that smoothe

toong, whose mu - sicke hell   can   moue.

The same is true of 'Thrice tosse these Oaken ashes.'
This ayre is conceived as a whole, cast in a perfect mood.
The uncertainty expressed in the words finds its counter-
part in the undulating melody of the piece. Though the
music appears to be written in the modern key of G minor, the absence of F sharp, the leading tone, gives the
melody the modal characteristic of medieval music. At
the same time, it emphasizes the mood of uncertainty
which characterizes the whole ayre.

Countless other ayres might be quoted along with their accompaniments to 'let well-tun'd words amaze with harmonie diuine,' though the accompaniments are extremely simple in most cases. Their main function was to fill in a harmony of fundamental chords, sometimes picking out a melody a third above or below a voice part for contrast. In the original lute parts, the accompaniment was thinner than the modern piano arrangement shown in the reproduction of 'Neuer Weather-beaten Saile' (Plate II), for instance, suggests. But an accompaniment could accentuate a mood. That was its *raison d'être*.

Thus the intimate relationship of music and poetry finds expression in rhythm, melody, and mood. With the development of these qualities, it was possible to point out some of the artistic skill of the musical poet. He may now be seen in his full stature.

Any consideration of Campion from the literary side, as a lyric poet; from the musical side, as a composer of ayres; reveals him as an artist. In his unique position as a true musical poet, expressing himself in his own peculiar idiom, he is a great figure. His success lies in a simple direct approach to the marriage of words and music. When considered technically as a poet, he is an arch experimentalist in meter. As a musical poet, he becomes a master of rhythmical cadences for the freedom of which he is indebted to his musical training. Closely allied to this mastery was his control of melodic line. This he secured by capturing both the sounds and the meanings of the words uttered with expression. His artistry was further enhanced by his fitting important words in the same position in each stanza so that they fell on the same notes with similar effect. Finally, he knew the pitch of feeling to which to set his ayres. All this was a subtle art—combining music and poetry which, as he said, 'will be much for him to doe that hath not power over both.' Sometimes it was a very subtle art. Campion tells the reader of the *Fourth Booke of Ayres* that 'the Apothecaries haue Bookes of Gold, whose leaves being opened are so light as that they are subiect to be shaken with the least breath, yet rightly handled, they serue both for ornament and vse; such are light Ayres.' But Campion was equal to his task.

Occasions arise, of course, when he is not always equally successful. He was seldom 'faultily faultless.' His faults may generally be attributed to a certain trait not uncommon among Elizabethans, that of starting something with enthusiasm and suffering a let-down before the work was completed; or, having conceived a total effect in the imagination, growing impatient with the details of its realization. So in the ayre 'It fell on a sommers day,' from *A Booke of Ayres*, a certain carelessness in setting the words and music is apparent. For example take this phrase and the words to two stanzas.

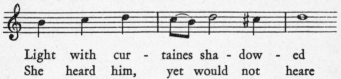

Light with cur - taines sha - dow - ed
She heard him, yet would not heare

Obviously the words of the second verse fail to fit the notes in the same proportion as in the first. Perhaps it might be better to state that the words of the second verse fit while those of the first are somewhat misproportioned.

Certainly, the parallelism of *curtaines* and *him yet* is a strange combination. Nor does *sha-dow-ed* fit well with *would not heare*. Such careless combination may be found in many ayres and thus take away the claim of impeccable fastidiousness for Campion. Usually, as in this case, the carelessness occurs when there are several verses. In this same ayre, Campion shows a mastery of caesural effect for three stanzas (at *) which is highly commendable. He spoils it in the final stanza not only by disregarding it completely, but also by stretching the words *euerie afternoon* out of all proportion in order to make an end of the stanza.

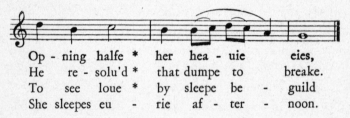

Op - ning	halfe	*	her	hea - uie	eies,
He	re - solu'd	*	that	dumpe to	breake.
To	see loue	*	by	sleepe be -	guild
She	sleepes eu	-	rie	af - ter -	noon.

Campion's ayre in sapphics, the only one included in the 1601 book, has often been cited as an unhappy venture. Its awkwardness, however, is not so apparent when it is considered as an ayre. Nor is this surprising in the light of the musical origin of many Greek meters. In this case Campion leaves the burden entirely to the complicated rhythm of the music. Note how insignificant the bar lines are and how the time-value of the notes dictates the rhythm of the melody.

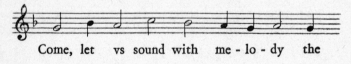

Come, let vs sound with me - lo - dy the

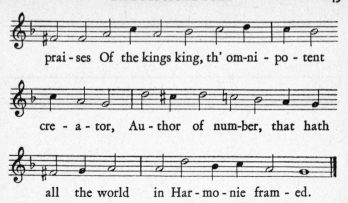

prai - ses Of the kings king, th' om-ni - po - tent
cre - a - tor, Au - thor of num-ber, that hath
all the world in Har - mo - nie fram - ed.

These, however, are minor errors in a collection of works notable for their artistic accomplishment. One side of the artist should not be overlooked: the improvements that he made in his own ayres. There are several examples, one of which occurs in the first of the *Two Bookes of Ayres*, 'The man of life vpright.' The wisdom of experience acquired in twelve years more or less may be seen in the changes in the words and the addition of a verse in comparing this ayre with that in the 1601 collection. The second musical setting profited by revision. On two occasions, Campion used the same setting for different words. The first of these appears rather strange. It is the setting of the second song in the *Lord Hayes Maske*, 'Moue now with measured sound,' written in a dancelike form which also serves for the ayre, 'The peaceful western wind' in the second of *Two Bookes of Ayres*. No evidence exists to tell which of these came first, and now that the origin of the tune has been questioned, further discussion seems useless. Noting their similarity is perhaps sufficient.

The second of these examples, the ayre 'Follow thy faire sun' has already been quoted, but it seems best to set it side by side with the later adaptation, 'Seeke the Lord,' in order to show how the same setting may be used, and used successfully for a different lyric. Bearing in mind all that has been said previously about rhythm, melody, and *especially mood*, it is, as we have seen in other examples, quite conceivable that these different lyrics as well as different verses may all find a place in the same tune.

Placing these ayres together in this fashion does rather suggest one point that has not been particularly emphasized. In the preceding chapter, the more specific ways in which music conditioned the Elizabethan lyric were dwelt upon. But when two different sets of words are found associated with the same music with such peculiar fitness, it implies that the words of at least one of these ayres must have been written second to the music. The same thing has happened, of course, in writing additional verses to a melody after the music to the first verse has been written. Under the circumstances in this situation, then, it is possible to see how definitely the three characteristics of music are linked to the same qualities of the words so that the words cannot be sung to any music but only to the music which agrees with the rhythm, melody, and mood inherent in, or lying behind, the words of the second lyric. These two ayres, as the illustrations graphically represent, are a definite proof of this phenomenon in every detail.

One point further is suggested in this connection. The musical poet in conceiving words and music simultane-

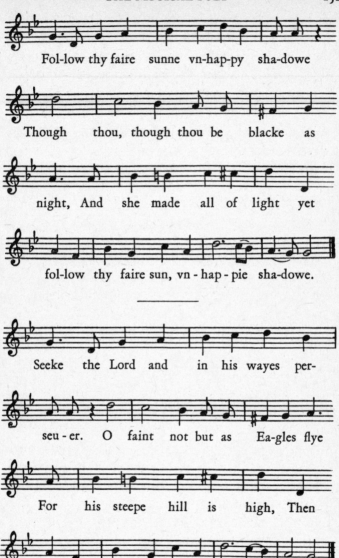

ously must have the tune constantly in his mind while he is composing the words of the entire lyric. Derived as the tune is from the inflections of the words in any of the verses, it must, therefore, spring from the same source at the time when the words first come to mind. Thus the rhythm and melody of both words and music become wedded within the same mood in the very process of creation.

In the preface to the *Fourth Booke of Ayres*, Campion says:

You may finde here some three or four Songs that haue beene published before, but for them, I referre you to the Players Bill, that is stiled *Newly reuiued, with Additions*, for you shall finde all of them reformed, eyther in Words or Notes . . . But if any squeamish stomachs shall checke at two or three vaine Ditties in the end of this Booke, let them powre off the clearest, and leaue those as dregs in the bottome. Howsoeuer, if they be but conferred with the *Canterbury Tales* of that venerable Poet *Chaucer*, they will then appeare toothsome enough.

Three songs appeared in the 1601 *Booke of Ayres*. Two of them are among the 'vaine Ditties' which, for the sake of the squeamish, are left for private investigation. The third, 'Loue me or not' will bear closer analysis. It is closely related to 'Follow your Saint' of the 1601 collection, but it does not have exactly the same setting.

'Follow your Saint' is one of Campion's finest lyrics and most perfect musical settings. Melted into one creation in the mould of the ayre, it becomes a rare work of art. Here the words and the notes are 'lovingly coupled together' with unusual effect. The majestic flowing rhythm, the pictorial melody, the sincerity of the mood,

X.

Ollow your Saint follow with accets sweet, There wrapt in cloud of
Haste you sad noates fall at her flying feete, But if she scorns my

sorrowe pitie moue, And tell the rauisher of my soule, I perish for her loue,
neuer ceasing paine, Then burst with sighing in her sight, And nere returne a gaine.

CANTVS.   **X.**

Oue me or not, loue her I must or dye,   O that her grace would my wishe
Leaue me or not, follow her needs must I.

comforts giue. How rich in her, how happy should I liue?

BASSVS.

PLATE I

all combine into a beautiful whole. This lyric made a profound impression on George Saintsbury, but he spoiled his praise by saying: 'What such a thing as this can want with an "air" it is difficult to say; it is very easy to see that the air, whatever it is, would have no little difficulty in matching the ineffable beauty of the prosodic accompaniment.' But Campion's ayres cannot be judged fairly without their music since words and notes are one and the same in the process of creation. In this case, incredible as it might seem to Mr. Saintsbury, the beauty is heightened by the music.

Now it is only the first phrase that was used in 'Loue me or not.' The remainder of this ayre is different, as the reproductions of the originals (Plate I) readily illustrate. That the words and notes of this phrase are appropriately matched when the mood of the ayre is considered cannot be denied. And it is such a happy musical phrase to use again if possible. Some resemblance might be forced out of the rest of the ayre by saying that the shorter of the two, 'Loue me or not,' called for a shortened melodic line, so that in 'Follow your Saint' there is an example of an augmented melody, and in 'Loue me or not' an example of melody in diminution. But the melodies are not sufficiently alike to descend to such details. Though 'Loue me or not' does not reach the 'purple heights' on which 'Follow your Saint' rests, it is, nevertheless, a fine ayre.

Several of Campion's finest ayres remain for more detailed consideration. Among these are: 'I care not for these Ladies,' 'There is a Garden in her face,' 'Author of light,' and 'Neuer weather-beaten Saile.'

The choice of 'I care not for these Ladies' makes it possible to summarize the various parts of this chapter by taking an ayre that has been frequently mentioned, and is, at the same time, recognized as one of the best.

I care not for these La - dies that must be
Give me kind A - ma - ryl - lis the wan - ton

woode   and   praide.   Na - ture arte dis-
coun - trey maide.

dain - eth; her   beau - tie is   her owne.   Her

when we court and kisse, she cries; for - sooth, let

go   But   when   we   come   where

com - fort is,   she   ne - uer will say no.

Following in the best tradition of the 'conditioned' Elizabethan lyric, the short stanza of six lines has an added four-line refrain which on each repetition grows more and more effective. The rhythmic phrasing is so closely allied with the melodic contour, even in little details of meaning such as the last line *she neuer will say no*, and both are so welded into the lightest of moods, that the three qualities of the more intimate relations of music and poetry are well illustrated. The original melody is reproduced in full here in its original notation without further comment.

The famous ayre 'There is a Garden in her face' in the *Fourth Booke of Ayres* has a charm which almost beggars description. The words recall a line of praise bestowed on Campion by Peele in his *Honour of the Garter* in 1593, when he thus hailed Campion:

thou
That richly cloth'st conceits with well made words.

Long has this lyric been recognized for its beauty, but how significantly increased is that beauty when the music is brought before the reader. Admittedly the first line, which is the title of the ayre, is nothing in itself besides an Elizabethan conceit. The melody of that line, however, is very impressive for the musical transcription of the word inflection.

There   is   a   Gar - den   in   her   face.

What the lyric can never bring is the effectiveness of the musical fantasia on the word 'cherry-ripe.' In all probability Campion has reproduced a London street cry here. The clever arrangement of the words might not in itself prove this, but the change in the tonality of the first repetition, contrasted with the first phrase, again with the second phrase, is ample evidence. Furthermore, the accompaniment is confined to chords before each cry, throwing it into relief in the manner suggestive of recitative.

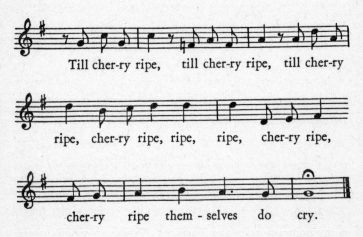

Till cher-ry ripe, till cher-ry ripe, till cher-ry ripe, cher-ry ripe, ripe, ripe, cher-ry ripe, cher-ry ripe them-selves do cry.

The original of the ayre is reproduced in the frontispiece.

In the first of *Two Bookes of Ayres* occurs an ayre not usually included among the lyrics culled from the song books, 'Author of light.' To find an explanation for its omission as a lyric would be difficult. As an ayre, it ranks with the best and is such an artistic creation that the skilful craftsmanship must not be overlooked. Here the master of rhythm, melody, and mood achieves great things. The melody begins after a chord of accompaniment and is notable for its close following of the words, for combined with the rhythm, which is very irregular, it produces a pictorial effect with comparative simplicity. Take such phrases as the following:

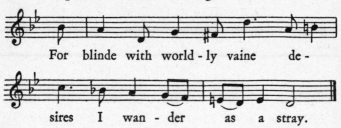

For blinde with world - ly vaine de -

sires I wan - der as a stray.

Outstandingly graphic are the settings of both verses to the next phrase. Note how the relative melodic positions of the *sunne* and *moone* to each other and to the *starres* and *under-lights* (degree lower on the staff) are indicated in this astrological line, and how the length of notes causes a rhythmic accent especially on *starres* after the preceding phrase. Again in the second stanza, note how perfectly counterpoised are *sinne* and *death*, *hell*, and *tempting fiends*, words contrasted with those of the first stanza. The setting called for the greatest care in the selection of the words in the second stanza to fit as perfectly as they do. The result is an ingenious combination, possibly the finest detail in all of Campion's ayres.

Sunne and Moone, Starres and un-der-lights I   see
Sinne and Death, Hell and temp-ting Fiends may rage.

The last musical phrase of the ayre is significant for its chromatic melody, an unusual procedure in the music of this period. Again it is an excellent illustration of placing important or contrasted words in the right positions.

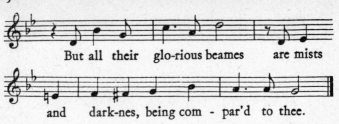

But all their glo-rious beames are mists and dark-nes, being com - par'd to thee.

Note here how excellently the primary advice to all modern song-writers is illustrated; namely, that if the sense of the words suggests ascent, then the melody must follow that inclination, and if it suggests descent, then the melody must do likewise. Thus *glorious beames* is high while *mists and darknes* low in pitch. The chromatics are a subtle touch to connote the search through darkness for light.

The majesty of the rhythm of the whole ayre is at once evident, yet how irregular is the phrasing. In the first illustration above, the phrase is long, coming between two shorter ones. The final phrase of the third illustration is the longest of all. Even in the slowest rhythms where it would seem natural to have phrases approximately equal, Campion has been most irregular. This is a fine example of the use of freedom in rhythm illustrating as it does a keen sensitiveness to its effectiveness. On the religious sincerity of the mood, it seems unnecessary to comment since its impressiveness is in itself sufficiently eloquent. The ayre is now given in its entirety.

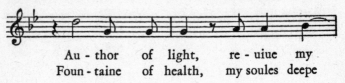

Au - thor   of light,   re - uiue my
Foun - taine of health, my soules deepe

dy - ing spright   Re - deeme   it from the
wounds re - cure,   Sweet showres of pi - ty

snares   of   all   con - found-ing night.
raine,   wash   my   vn - clean-ness pure

Lord,   light   me   to thy   bless - ed
One   drop   of   thy de - sir - ed

way; for blinde, for blinde with world-ly vaine   de-
grace, the faint, the faint and fad - ing hart   can

sires   I   wan - der   as   a   stray
raise   and   in   ioyes   bo - some place

Sunne and Moone, Starres and un - der lights   I
Sinne and Death, Hell   and temp-ting Fiends may

see,   But   all   their   glo - rious beames
rage   but God   his   owne   will   guard

are mists and dark- nes being com-par'd to thee
and their sharp paines and griefe in time as-swage

From the same collection which contains 'Author of Light' comes the last selection, 'Neuer weather-beaten Saile.' It is reproduced in its modern dress in the accompanying illustration. Like its companion ayre, it is cast in a religious mood which transcends an equally successful coupling of the words and notes in a more regular rhythmic setting. The details of the rhythmic and melodic writing are now sufficiently well known to be readily perceived. The repetition of the phrase, *O come quickly*, which occurs only once in the reprint of the words, is notable for increasing the religious fervour and giving a more vivid expression to the plaintive meaning behind the whole. Attention should be called to the modern transcription of the lute tablature, entirely the discovery of Dr. Fellowes, which is harmonically fuller than the original accompaniment in order to cope with modern ears and instruments. For sheer beauty of sound, this ayre is one of the most outstanding of them all (Plate II).

The story of the marriage of words and music in Campion's ayres has now been told as thoroughly as any creative process may be divulged. It is the melody derived from the inflection of the spoken words that outlines the ayre, the rhythmic phrasing suggested by the flow of the words that gives it life, and the mood which transmutes the emotional meaning behind the words into sound that makes the union complete. To perceive this in Campion is not only to demonstrate the reciprocal relations existing between music and verse which bring spontaneity to the Elizabethan lyric, but also to reveal the secret of successful song-writing. From all this creative activity,

NEVER WEATHER–BEATEN SAIL

S. & B. 8290

PLATE II

Campion emerges a great and human artist for he had learned the secret that could be known only in an age in which the air rang with music, an age in which the people were endowed with a musical consciousness, an age when the lyric impulse joined itself with music and flew through the world on the wings of song.

VIII

THE POET AS MUSICIAN

THAT Campion is, of course, as excellent a composer of music as he is of lyrics might be expected if the union of the two was fully comprehended. The greater is the pity, then, that the music was ever divorced from the words. To appreciate this misfortune it may be well to know some of the requirements of sixteenth-century musical composition as promulgated by Thomas Morley, the first Englishman to write an important treatise on musical theory. A large share of his 'rules to be obserued in dittying' were naturally closely followed by Campion. Since the statement of those rules is related in part to a description of Campion's music, and may be considered a summary of his practice in composing, the following observations are quoted at some length.

Dispose your musicke according to the nature of the words which you are therein to express, as whatsoeuer matter it be which you haue in hand, such a kind of musicke must you frame to it . . . For, it will be a great absurditie to vse a sad harmonie to a merrie matter, or a merrie harmonie to a sad lamentable or tragicall dittie. You must then when you would expresse any word signifying hardness, crueltie, bitternesse and other such like, make the harmonie like vnto it, that is, somewhat harsh and hard but yet so yt offend not. Likewise, when any of your words shal expresse complaint, dolor, repentance, sighs, teares and such like, let your harmonie be sad and doleful.

The light musicke hath beene of late more deepely diued into, so that there is no uanitie which in it hath not beene followed to the full . . . If therefore you will compose in this kind, you must possesse your selfe with an amorous humor (for in no co[m]position shal you proue admirable except you put on, and possesse your selfe wholy with that vaine wherein you compose) so that you must in your musicke be wauering like the wind, sometime wanton, sometime drooping, sometime graue and staide, otherwhile effeminat, . . . and the more varietie you shew the better shal you please.

Also, if the subiect be light, you must cause your musicke to go in motions, which carrie with them a celeritie or quicknesse of time, as minimes, crotchets and quauers: if it be lamentable, the note must goe in slow and heauie motions, as semibreues, breues, and such like, and of all of this you shall finde examples euerie where in the workes of the good musicians. Moreouer, you must haue a care that when your matter signifieth ascending, high heauen, and such like, you make your musicke ascend: and by the contrarie where your dittie speaketh of descending lowenes, depth, hell, and others such, you must make your musicke descend . . . We must also haue a care so to applie the notes to the wordes, as in singing there be no barbarisme committed: that is, that we cause no sillable which is by nature short be expressed by manie notes or one long note, nor no long sillable bee expressed with a shorte note, but in this fault do the practicioners erre more grosselie, then in any other . . . Lastlie, you must not make a close (especiallie a full close) till the full sence of the words be perfect: so that keeping these rules you shall haue a perfect agreement, and as it were a harmonicall concent betwixt the matter and the musicke, and likewise you shall bee perfectly vnderstoode of the auditor what you sing, which is one of the highest desgrees of praise, which a musicion in dittying can attaine vnto or wish for.

That Campion observed the first counsels is immediately apparent after noting the examples of the preceding chapter. On one point, however, he differed from Morley: that of expressing the nature of every word by the music. His sentiments on this are probably set forth in the 1601 preface where it states:

> But there are some, who to appeare the more deepe, and singular in their iudgement, will admit no Musicke but . . . where the nature of euerie word is precisely exprest in the Note, like the old exploided action in Comedies, where if they did pronounce *Memeni*, [*sic*], they would point to the hinder part of their heads, if *Video*, put their finger in their eye. But such childish obseruing of words is altogether ridiculous, and we ought to maintaine as well in Notes, as in action a manly cariage, gracing no word, but that which is eminent, and emphaticall.

Certainly Campion's music is on the whole free from decorative or flowering writing—a style which was more popular with the madrigal composers and Morley himself who, not content with musical ornamentation derived from words, indulged in *fa la la* refrains. There are, of course, occasional places where the new idea was not followed by Campion. This is illustrated in the phrase,

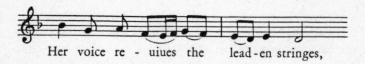

Her voice re - uiues the   lead-en stringes,

where he tried to convey the idea of reviving in the undulating curve of the eighth and sixteenth notes.

In the phrase quoted below, the word *heauie* is given

the eighth-note group to suggest the physical exertion of opening sleepy eyes.

Op - ning halfe   her   hea - uie   eies.

These instances, however, are few. Much of the simplicity and directness of his music comes from Campion's adherence to this new principle; namely, of leaving to the rhythm, melody, and mood of the whole ayre the true expression of the words.

In the more general matter of musical phrases ascending and descending in accordance with the meaning of the words which Morley picturesquely outlined in the above quotation, Campion followed the old principle. The rule is one of the strictest for a successful setting of words and music even today. The illustrations which have already been given in the preceding chapter from such ayres as 'Follow your Saint,' 'Awake, awake, thou heauy spright,' and especially 'Author of Light,' explain this in detail.

But it is in the last matter, that of not making a final cadence 'til the full sence of the words be perfect,' that Campion excelled. He knew the limits of effectiveness in this short form and had mastered the art of making musical cameos. Aside from his knowledge of the right proportioning of rhythm, melody, and mood to capture the effect desired—development of which has also been discussed in Chapter VII—Campion made particular use of the device of repeated word phrases in the form of musical sequences. While, as we have said, in the madrigal these repetitions were part of the form of the composition and were of a rhythmical character, in the ayre they were used primarily to make perfect the full sense of the words.

So in 'Mistris, Beauty, since you so desire' in the 1601 collection and the *Fourth Booke of Ayres*, the point rests in the use of the three sequences of the phrase

But a little higher.

This was further illustrated in 'Neuer Weather-beaten Saile' in the phrase 'O come quickly,' and again in 'When to her lute Corrina sings' where the ayre gains in solidity by the repetitions not only of *her sighes*, but also *the strings do breake*.

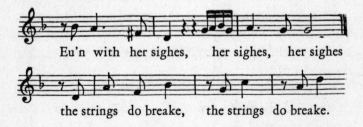

Eu'n with her sighes, her sighes, her sighes

the strings do breake, the strings do breake.

Many other illustrations could be given of this device which is a favourite with Campion. One pleasant ayre, 'Sweet, exclude mee not,' perhaps deserves quotation for the delightful way in which Campion wrote a fuller meaning into his musical sequences. The phrase, *yet a little more*, is cleverly set in a descending line of music to denote the persuasive inflection implied in the meaning of the lyric as a whole. On repetition, the sequence is raised one whole step to portray increased ardour. Finally, in the third repetition in order to give a sense of even greater persuasiveness, Campion changed his eighth-note phrasing, so rearranging the time-values as to convey the culmination of feeling that the repetitions signify.

Sweet, ex-clude mee not, nor be di - uid -

ed from him that ere long must bed thee:

All thy maid-en doubts Law hath de - cid - ed;

Sure we are, and I must wed thee.

Pre - sume then yet a lit - tle more,

yet a lit - tle more, yet a lit - tle more,

yet a lit - tle more, Here's the

way, the way, the way, barre not the dore.

It might be well to compare this ayre with 'Beauty since you so desire,' quoted in Chapter VI, to observe a subtle variation in Campion's technique. Where in the latter ayre the sequence *but a little higher* was handled in a similar way to *yet a little more*, it did not have the additional line to give a still further meaning by another repetition. The connotation of this final line of the ayre quoted above is sufficiently supplied, in the way it has been recorded musically by Campion, to imply the full meaning without further explanation.

The opening ayre in the *Third Booke of Ayres*, 'Oft haue I sighed' is a slight thing. As a lyric it amounts to just a few lines:

Oft haue I sigh'd for him that heares me not;
Who absent hath both loue and mee forgot.
O yet I languish still through his delay:
Dayes seeme as yeares when wisht friends breake their day.

Had hee but lou'd as common louers vse,
His faithlesse stay some kindnesse would excuse:
O yet I languish still, still constant mourne
For him that can breake vowes but not returne.

But as an ayre, it takes on a substance that gives it ineffable charm illustrating, at the same time, not only the place of music in the creation of words and the place of the words in the creation of the music of the ayres, but also how the expression of emotion can be added through music. In spite of the slightness of its material, this ayre is a superb example of the greatness of Campion's art.

Oft haue I sigh'd, oft haue I sigh'd, oft haue I sigh'd for him that heares me not; Who ab-sent hath both loue and mee for-got. O yet I lan-guish still, yet I lan-guish still, yet I lan-guish still through his de-lay: dayes seem as yeares when wisht friends breake their day.

The effects are derived from the repetitions. In other examples these have been fairly strict but there is much variation in these sequences and subtleties that heighten the effect while helping to expand the meaning contained in the words. Here the sighs are expressed in the conventional manner by the rest between phrases, but a delicate touch of meaning is given the second repetition by the shortening of the note-values. The descending chromatic phrases that denote languishing, however, are a remarkably artistic achievement in the art of perfectly communicating the meaning of the words in the sound of the music. Each sequence of the phrase *O yet I languish still* varies slightly in its musical material to express the meaning while again the rest between sequences prolongs the idea. Finally, the whole tenor of the ayre is summed up in the three-note phrases at the end where the music is carrying still further the thought of sighing while the reason is given out in the final words.

Campion's music is essentially melodic but he did not write melodies as Schubert and his contemporaries wrote them. As was pointed out in the first chapter, Schubert's melodies were the result of an impulse of refinement. They had an intrinsic musical value of their own which made it possible to separate them from the words, as Liszt did in making his piano transcriptions, and have them musically significant. Campion, like most Elizabethans, wrote melodic outlines rather than melodies, considered from the modern point of view. In the seventh chapter, we learned that these melodic outlines had their origin in the inflections of the words, that they were projections of the sound of spoken poetry into musical notation. Hence, they do not stand up musically in the same way as Schubert's melodies. Campion's melodies belong to the words. Much of the beauty of his music lies in the suavity of the melodic contours that seem to be part of the vocal expression of the verse. In many ways these melodies are reminiscent of the simple, natural melodies of English folk-tunes. Their freedom, freshness, and lightness, as well as the method of their creation, are characteristic of early English music. They are, however, more refined than the folk-song melodies and because of this are more appealing. Campion had a flair for a neatly turned phrase. The appropriateness of the line,

There is a Gar - den in her face.

rising as it does out of the inflection of the words, has its purely musical value in the rise to the major third on *Gar*den. Such phrases as

And clouds their storms dis-

charge Up - on the ay - rie towres,

or

To his sweet lute A -

pol - lo sung the mo-tions of the Spheares,

appeal not only because of the excellent pictorial treatment of the descending and ascending line of the first, and the undulating curve to denote the motive of the spheres in the second, but simply because of their musical sound. In just satisfying the ear, they achieve an effect for which many a musician earnestly strives.

Then having hit on a happy phrase, Campion will often be found using it for several lines of verse, as we have seen on several occasions. This occurs most frequently in the repetition of the first phrases of ayres. For example:

In such matters, the two important points which must be recognized have already been pointed out but will be repeated for emphasis. The first, that of finding the right words to fit the music which went so successfully with the first line, depends either on the sequence of production: the words and music coupled in the first stanza, then the probable setting of the words to the music in the second; or, the simultaneous creation of the whole in the mind of the musical poet. The second, that a tune may be used for several sets of words, is wholly dependent on the proper perspective of the relations of rhythm, melody, and mood in both words and notes, which was the subject of the preceding chapter. Often tempo has a good deal to do with a successful comprehension of the union of words and music. This is true of the ayre 'Faine would I wed,' Campion's longest effort in song. In this, each phrase is repeated once to different words, then this form is itself repeated six times. The rapid tempo in which the ayre is sung makes everything seem rightly placed. If the parts of an ayre seem to be haphazardly thrown together, then probably the mood of the whole will be the deciding factor. Campion recognized all these principles. His ayres reflect his insight into their possibilities.

The accompaniments written for these ayres have not entered much into this discussion because they appear to be of secondary importance, though they are an intrinsic part of the whole composition. Usually the simplest harmonies are used to lend colour by bringing a satisfying fulness of sound as a background to the melody, or to fill out the rhythm, or to cast the spell of a mood. Campion's accompaniments are simple because the harmony of the early seventeenth century was still in its infancy. They are predominantly tonic and dominant with the chief emphasis on the tonic. The tonalities are restricted principally to the keys of C, and G major or G minor. Occasionally other keys are present in his music, but the most common final chord is built on the bass note G. Of course, keys as they are recognized today had not been formulated at this time. Instead, the modal characteristics of medieval music still left a faint trace of influence in Elizabethan music.

These accompaniments unquestionably sounded far more effective on the lute for which they were designed than they do on the piano in their modern transcriptions. If in these transcriptions the music sounds somewhat strange, this is partly owing to this modal characteristic in English music before 1600. On the whole, the effect is pleasing and distinctly individual. It enhances more than it detracts from the music. In addition, the strangeness may arise from what appears to be a total lack of a feeling for modulation. Abrupt changes of major and minor chords, cross relations, and other sudden shifts of tonality are all part of Elizabethan music. But modulation as now conceived could not exist since there was no standardized system of keys. Yet withal, a quaint charm is present in Campion's music that transcends these apparent barbarisms.

Music was in a transitional stage. In Campion there seems to be as much of the old as there is of the new, which fact makes his music all the more interesting. For exactly the same reason his treatise on music assumes a significance that cannot be overlooked. It, too, marks the transition by retaining sufficient of the old to make a firm foundation for building up a new theory.

Although the *Observations in the Art of English Poesie* suffered an eclipse almost immediately after publication, Campion's second prose treatise, *A New Way of Making Fowre Parts in Counter-point*, became, on the other hand, one of the most important works on music published during the seventeenth century. Originally written about 1618, it was not issued in a second edition until 1655. Reasons for this interval between editions may be discovered in the general social unrest and decline of artistic activity in England during this time. But having been published again, the treatise was at once incorporated by John Playford into his *Introduction to the Skill of Musick* in 1660, under the heading 'The Art of Discant.' Placed in this work as a distinct addition, it reappeared regularly in the various editions of Playford until 1683. It was finally replaced by a newly corrected and revised section in the twelfth edition in 1694. The editor of this new section was none other than the distinguished musician Henry Purcell. From this brief account of its history, we may judge that the work was not only considered to have merit, but also to be sufficiently sound to compete favourably with the new ideas coming into music during the latter part of the century.

As a matter of fact, this treatise of Campion was of immediate value because it pointed the way to writing in four-part harmony by suggesting the construction of chords with their foundations in the bass. It promoted a

feeling for key tonalities. Finally, it counselled composers against false relations, consecutive fifths, and octaves,
all of which are pitfalls for every beginner in the study
of harmony and counterpoint.

All this was a definite step away from the polyphonic
style of music which dominated Elizabeth's reign, where,
no matter how many parts were sung, the music was conceived horizontally as so many melodies agreeing at certain points by courtesy, only to pass through them and
not pause for a harmonic effect. With Campion, a pause
for a harmonic effect, perceived vertically at the point of
agreement, was recognized. Thus the idea of progression
from chord to chord arose. Campion was the first to
record the transition. A parallel movement was under
way on the continent, especially in Italy, but Campion
first realized its significance for the English. The recognition of this principle makes his treatise second only in
importance to Morley's *Plaine and Easie Introduction to
Practical Musick* among books on musical theory in England.

Until Campion's treatise was written, the only significant English work on musical theory was that of Morley
in 1597. Written in the quaint form of a dialogue, it is
a readable book that gently involves the reader in a thorough technical discussion of the art of descant and composition. It is chiefly devoted to instruction in the contrapuntal writing of motets and madrigals. Though of
considerable value as a manual for study, the book is
diffuse because of its style. Campion, on the other hand,
following the same methods displayed in his *Observations*,
is more practical because of his clear, straight-forward

style and his brevity. This quality, then, in addition to his understanding of the trend of the new music which made his book valuable to Playford, adds considerable stature to his work. Therefore, when Campion pauses in the midst of his essay on counterpoint to say

If I should discouer no more then this already deciphered of Counter-point . . . might I be mine owne Iudge, I had effected more in Counter-point, then any man before me hath euer attempted.[1]

he is not making the rash pretensions to his position as a musical theorist that some critics might like to point out. There is a certain amount of theory that is common to all musicians. In so far as this knowledge could be known to both Campion and Morley, it does not follow that Campion necessarily used Morley's work as a source. Indeed, Campion was going beyond Morley in setting up new rules for four-part counterpoint. This in itself justifies his boastful statement.

In the dedication of this treatise, Campion states that the purpose of writing was to elucidate the whole business of composition, 'contenting my selfe onely with a poore, and easie inuention; yet new and certaine; by which the skill of Musicke shall be redeemed from much darknesse, wherein enuious antiquitie did inuolue it.' He expected some rudimentary knowledge of music on the part of his readers as the nature of his preface would indicate. Here will be found his remarks on the singing

1. In his introduction (p.lxv), Vivian finds himself unable to concede the claims made by Campion in this passage. Vivian was apparently unaware of the transition through which music was passing at the time.

of the scale which in his time was six notes. Campion advocated a grouping of four notes which resembled the Greek tetrachords. Our modern scale of eight notes was derived from joining two of these tetrachords together. Campion thus sensed the modern development of the scale.

The significance of the first section 'Of Counterpoint' is Campion's recognition that 'the Base is the foundation of the other three parts' in music. His whole approach to the subject is given in the title of the work, *Of Making Fowre Parts in Counter-point*. He builds them from bass notes. This perception that 'the Base containes in it both the Aire and true iudgement of the key' is Campion's contribution. Morley in this respect was more inclined to follow the ancients who 'tooke their sight [intervals between parts] from the Tenor which was rather done out of necessity then any respect to the true nature of Musicke.' The exposition which follows this ruling about the bass part is a simple lesson in elementary counterpoint for four voices not unlike that given today. An interested reader would find it lucid and instructive. Its importance lies in the fact that by drawing attention to a formal bass as the foundation of everything, Campion thus chains the other parts to a movement in accordance with a definite scheme of intervals (of the third, fifth, and eighth) reckoned from the bass. Thus the idea of chord progressions based on a succession of bass notes is established. *This is elementary harmony.* Here, then, are old and new together, since the counterpoint of four voices harnessed to a bass now becomes the harmony of common chords in its most elemental state. Yet in this simple state, it is harmony adaptable to good four-part singing, the kind of singing which was so fashionable after the Restoration.

In recognizing the 'Tones of Musicke,' which is the subject of the second section of the treatise, Campion stated an important principle that lies at the foundation of all modern music.

Of all things that belong to the making vp of a Musition, the most necessary and vsefull for him is the true knowledge of the Key or Moode, or Tone, for all signifie the same thing, with the closes belonging vnto it, for there is no tune that can haue any grace or sweetnesse, vnlesse it be bounded within a proper key, without running into strange keyes which haue no affinity with the aire of the song.

Campion's idea was to have composers observe strictly the tonal limits of the key in which they wrote by establishing those keys by a definite set of rules. Today this seems a very simple matter, but in Campion's day the tunes were often 'begun in one key and ended in another quite contrary to nature,' and no one hearing them could determine just where things began or ended. Morley made a similar observation:

For euery key hath a peculiar ayre proper vnto it selfe, so that if you goe into another then that wherein you begun, you change the aire of the song, which is as much as to wrest a thing out of his nature, making the asse leape vpon his maister and the Spaniell bears the loade.

But Morley had no rules for keeping in the same key. It remained for the composer to contrive to do this as well as he could. Campion proceeded to show how it could be done.

The third and final section, 'Of the Taking of all Concords, perfect and imperfect,' which Campion based on a treatise by Sethus Calvisius, a contemporary German astronomer and chronologer, is devoted to an exposition of simple contrapuntal practice which is not germane to our study. One remark is worth noting since it is advice which Campion often followed himself:

He that will be diligent to know, and carefull to obserue the true allowances, may be bolde in his composition, and shall proue quickly ready in his sight, doing safely and resolutely that which others attempt tymerously and vncertainely.

———

The treatise, however brief it may be, assumes an important place in the history of musical theory in the light of these observations. It is a typical work of Campion in its conciseness and practicality. Its intrinsic value was recognized by its use throughout the century.

The foregoing discussion devoted to a consideration of the musical side of Campion's work was intended to acquaint the reader with the thoroughness and the significance of the poet as a musician. During the discussion of the musical treatise the poet necessarily stood very much in the background. But now he resumes his co-partnership with the musician and becomes a writer of masques. If Campion as a writer of ayres must be recognized as a musical poet, then as a writer of masques, he is a true poet-musician. In both cases he is ever conscious of the marriage of poetry and music. But in the masques even more than in the ayres, it was music that led Campion to create a form which, while it followed in the tradition of a century or so, was, nevertheless, an individual triumph for him.

Though closely allied with literature, the masque hardly acquired its full literary characteristics until after Campion. From 1613, its literary value may be said to have increased under the influence of its greatest adherent, Ben Jonson. Before this time the general occupation of the masque had been that of a musical entertainment at court with only the pleasure of the moment in mind. The masque, therefore, was only incidentally literature and primarily entertainment. When Campion wrote in 1607, it was still in a somewhat indeterminate form. By 1614, its character was changed through an attempt to comply with the demands of King James who cared little for music and much for dramatic display, and through the art of Ben Jonson.

It is inevitable that in any treatment of the masque Jonson should assume first place among the masque writers. But Campion ranks a close second. Fundamentally the two were opposed in their attitude toward the form and purpose of the masque. Jonson conceived it first with a dramatic sense, then with a lyric gift, and finally with some appreciation of the place of music therein. His chief responsibility was to write a libretto. There were plenty of talented musicians and stage directors to complete the work as a dramatic entertainment.

With Campion it was different. He conceived a masque to be a musical festival with songs and dances of many varieties. Its dramatic value was of little import. His credo, far different from that of Jonson, is stated at the end of his *Description of a Maske in honour of the Lord Hayes* as follows:

> *Neither buskin now, nor bayes*
> *Challenge I; a Ladies prayse*
> *Shall content my proudest hope.*
> *Their applause was all my scope;*
> *And to their shrines properly*
> *Reuels dedicated be:*
> *Whose soft eares none ought to pierce*
> *But with smooth and gentle verse.*

His three masques testify to a fancy for spectacular musical extravaganzas where poetic imagination was allowed to run riot. The sky, with clouds, was literally the limit, and the aim was to please. He was true to the tradition of the masque in his keen attention to the music. In comparison with Jonson, Campion's masques seem loosely thrown together, attaining unity only by sheer lyric genius and lavish pageantry. But Campion was evidently content with the spontaneity and variety that he brought to his creations. Jonson could never have given the same amount of attention to music and his object was usually more than just to entertain. Granting, then, that there are two points of view here, Campion's position is one of considerable importance.

The complicated history of the development of the masque need not be set down here in full. Until the last decade of the sixteenth century there had been little advancement over the dancing pageant of the maskers at court entertainments. Interest in the masque was probably stimulated at the Inns of Court about 1595 when

Davison's *Masque of Proteus* was given. At this time a
taste for dramatic interest may be detected. Jonson's first
masque in 1605, the *Masque of Blacknesse*, was an imma-
ture affair, but it contained the embryo of the dramatic
development which came in later years. Then, on Twelfth
Night 1607, came Campion's *Lord Hayes Maske*. Its performance is significant in throwing light on the contemporary estimation in which Campion must have been
held at the time. For the occasion was an auspicious one.
'The marriage . . . took place under the immediate favour and countenance of the king, with whom Sir James
Hay had long been in high favour.' The masque is unique
for its unusual attention to musical effects. On St. Valen-
tine's day 1613, for no less an occasion than the marriage
of the Princess Elizabeth, Campion was again called upon.
Ben Jonson was abroad at the time. Campion responded
with his *Lords Maske* which was given as the first of three
to celebrate the festivities. Shortly afterward he wrote
'A Relation of the late Royall Entertainment given by
the Right Honorable the Lord Knowles at Cawsome-
House neere Redding: to our most Gracious Queene,
Queene Anne.' This was more like an example of a
masque of the last century. Then in December of that
same year, Campion composed the so-called *Squires Maske*
for the marriage of the Earl of Somerset and the divorced
Countess of Essex, at which king, queen, prince, and
nobility were present. These, then, are Campion's works
as a masque writer. The importance of the events sur-
rounding each presentation shows clearly that his abil-
ities were highly esteemed.

Historically, these masques are important as precursors

of English opera. Although continental influences were forceful in moulding the opera of the Restoration, the form, however cloaked it was in the colourful garments of Italy, was nevertheless English. Its ancestry can be traced back through at least two centuries of the English love for music, the early dramas, and these court entertainments. The 1607 masque is particularly significant for the marked interest that is shown in the music, an interest so keen that the masque seems to be all song and dance. One innovation is important: this masque is probably the first in which songs in the form of a dialogue appear. The dialogue

> *Who is the happier of the two,*
> *A maid, or wife?*
> *Which is more to be desired,*
> *Peace or strife?*

is thus the first example. The music is unfortunately not available though it is based on the marriage song 'Now hath Flora,' which is quoted later in a sketch of this masque. The connection of this dialogue song with operatic musical form is obvious.

Another important thread of development may be discerned in the *Lords Maske* of 1613. After a boisterous dance by the anti-maskers the description runs:

But in the end thereof the musick changed into a very solemne ayre which they softly played *while Orpheus spake.*

This must have been an attempt at recitative which flourished in Restoration opera. That the recitative should come in music after the reduction of voice parts from the madrigal to the solo of the ayre does not seem unusual. A single voice singing to an accompaniment might become still more simplified to a melodic line with an occasional chord of accompaniment. This of course is recitative. All the materials for native opera were, then, present in Campion's masques in the development of English music at the turn of the century. That the growth was stunted by foreign influences is another matter. But Campion's masques show all the tendencies.

Before considering in detail the *Lord Hayes Maske* which so perfectly illustrates the poet-musician at work, it might be well to glance at the others. Certain features are characteristic of all three masques: the dance finale, the transformation scenes, the use of music to drown out the stage machinery, the anti-masque, etc. The dance of course was the *raison d'être* of the whole entertainment. At the end of the masque Campion planned at least three separate dances. The *Lords Maske* is interesting for the closely knitted relation between the dancing and the singing. After their first dance 'while they [the maskers] breath, the time is entertained with a dialogue song.' The words at the beginning of the song are addressed to the dancers.

> *Breath you now, while Io Hymen*
> *To the Bride we sing.*

After the second dance:

> *Breathe againe, while we with musicke*
> *Fill the emptie space:*

During the dialogue, however, a custom was followed that was as old as the court entertainment itself. It was as follows:

The Maskers during this Dialogue take out others to daunce with them, men women, and women men, and first of all the Princely Bridegroome and Bride were drawne into these solemne Reuels, which continued a long space.

Last came the 'dance triumphant' of the Maskers and the final exit.

Campion must have particularly liked transformation scenes. He uses them both extensively and elaborately. An interesting passage occurs at the beginning of the *Squires Maske* which is worth quoting.

In ancient times, when any man sought to shadowe or heighten his Inuention, he had a store of feyned persons readie for his purpose; as *Satyres, Nymphes*, and their like . . . But in our dayes, although they haue not vtterly lost their vse, yet finde they so little credit, that our moderne writers haue rather transferred their fictions to the persons of Enchaunters and Commaunders of spirits . . . In imitation of them . . . I grounded my whole Inuention upon Inchauntmens and several transformations.

Campion's stage was always divided into an upper and lower part allowing all the more space for invention. With the use of this device, a performance such as the following was possible.

Then out of the ayre a cloude descends, discouering six of the Knights alike . . . and withall on either side of the Cloud, on the two Promontories, the other sixe Maskers are sodainly transformed out of pillars of golde; at which time, while they come forward to the dancing-place, this Chorus is sung, and on a sodaine the whole Sceane is changed: for where as before all seemed to be done at the sea and sea coast, now the Promontories are sodainly remoued, and London with the Thames is very arteficially presented in their place.

Because of the almost inconceivable elaboration that these scenic ideas must have called forth, the most spectacular description in the *Lords Maske* is given at some length in Campion's own words to add to the general effect.

In the end of the first part of this Song, the vpper part of the Scene was discouered by the sodaine fall of a curtaine; then in clowdes of seuerall colours (the vpper part of them being fierie, and the middle heightned with siluer) appeared eight Starres of extraordinarie bignesse, which were so placed, as that they seemed to be fixed betweene the Firmament and the Earth.

This song follows shortly:

> *Aduance you Chorall motions now*
> *You musick-louing lights:*
> *This night concludes the nuptiall vow,*
> *Make this the best of nights:*
> *So brauely Crowne it with your beames*
> *That it may liue in fame*
> *As long as* Rhenus *or the* Thames
> *Are knowne by either name.* etc.

According to the humour of this Song, the Starres mooued in an exceeding strange and delightfull manner, and I suppose fewe haue euer seene more neate artifice, then Master *Innigoe Iones* shewed in contriuing their Motion . . . About the end

of this Song, the Starres suddainely vanished, as if they had
been drowned amongst the Cloudes, and the eight Maskers
appeared in their habits . . . The ground of their attires
was massie Cloth of Siluer, embossed with flames of Embroid-
ery; on their heads, they had Crownes, Flames made all of
Gold-plate Enameled, and on top a Feather of Silke, representing a cloude of smoake. Vpon their new transformation, the
whole Scoene being Cloudes dispersed, and there appeared
an Element of artificiall fires, with seuerall circles of lights, in
continuall motion, representing the house of Prometheus.

The use of music to hide the squeaking 'Ingins' is illustrated shortly after the above spectacle:

From the side of the Scoene appeared a bright and transparent
cloud, which reached from the top of the heauens to the earth:
on this cloud the Maskers led by Prometheus descended with
the musick of a full song.

But since the *Lord Hayes Maske* embodies every fanciful
offshoot of a poetic imagination to which is added a musician's fancy, a glimpse at the result of the fusion of the
two may serve to introduce the master of two arts in his
unrestrained glory. The opening description, again given
in Campion's phraseology, will make a good framework
for this sketch.

The greate hall (wherein the Maske was presented) received
this diuision, and order: The vpper part where the cloth &
chaire of State were plac't, had scaffoldes and seates on eyther
side continued to the skreene; right before it was made a
partition for the dauncing place; on the right hand whereof
were consorted ten Musitions, with Basse and Meane Lutes,
a Bandora, a double Sackbott, and an Harpsicord, with two
treble Violins; on the other side somewhat neerer the skreene
were plac't 9 Violins and three Lutes, and to answere both
the Consorts (as it were in a triangle) six Cornets, and six

Chappell voyces, were seated almost right against them, in a place raised higher in respect of the pearcing sound of those Instruments: eighteene foote from the skreen, an other Stage was raised higher by a yearde then that which was prepared for dancing: This higher Stage was all enclosed with a double vale, so artificailly painted, that it seemed as if dark cloudes had hung before it: within that shrowde was concealed a greene valley, with greene trees round about it, and in the midst of them nine golden trees of fifteene foote high, with arms and braunches very glorious to behold: From the which groue toward the State was made a broad descent to the daunc- ing place, iust in the midst of it; on either hand were two ascents, like the two sides of hilles, drest with shrubbes and trees; that on the right hand leading to the bowre of *Flora*: the other to the house of *Night*; which bowre and house were plac't opposite at either end of the skreene, and betweene them both was raised a hill, hanging like a cliffe ouer the groue belowe and on the top of it a goodly large tree was set . . .

At once the reader perceives the detailed attention that is given in order to procure the most suitable arrange- ment of the musical instruments so that the tone qualities will be properly balanced. The setting has been designed for specific purposes as well as to make a striking pic- ture. At a time when the Elizabethan drama was given in theatres without scenery, such an effect as this must have made a great impression.

As soone as the King was entred the great Hall, the Hoboyes (out of the wood on the top of the hill) entertained the time till his Maiestie and his trayne were placed, and then after a little expectation the consort of ten began to play an Ayre, at the sound whereof the vale on the right hand was with- drawne, and the ascent of the hill with the bower of *Flora* was

discouered, where *Flora* & *Zepherus* were busily plucking flowers from the Bower, and throwing them into two baskets,
which two *Siluans* held . . . As soone as the baskets were
filled, they came downe . . . toward the dauncing place,
the consort of tenne ceac't, and the foure *Siluans* [with two
meane Lutes, a base Lute, and a Bandora] playd the same Ayre,
to which *Zepherus* and the two other *Siluans* did sing . . .
and going vp and downe as they song, they strowed flowers
all about the place.

Now   hath   Flo - ra   robde her bowers
Flow - ers with bri-   dals well agre:

to   be - frend this   place with flowres,
fresh as brides and Bridegroomes be.

strow a - bout strow a - bout the
strow a - bout strow a - bout and

skie rainde neuer kind - li - er showers,
mixe them with fitte mel - o - die,

earth hath no prince - lier flowers

the[n] ro - ses white and ro - ses

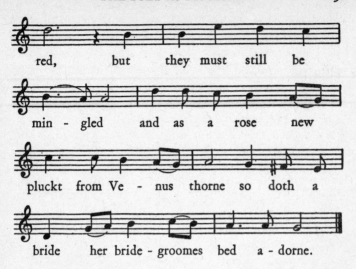

red, but they must still be
min - gled and as a rose new
pluckt from Ve - nus thorne so doth a
bride her bride - groomes bed a - dorne.

Flora speaks on the occasion of the marriage, and then the dialogue song follows.

This song being ended the whole vale is sodainly drawne, the groue and trees of gold, and the hill of *Dianas* tree are at once discouered. Night appeares in her house with her 9 houres, apparrelled in large robes of black taffatie, painted thick with starres, their haires long, blacke, and spangled with gold, on their heads coronets of stars, and their faces blacke. Euery hour bore in his hand a blacke torch, painted with starres, and lighted.

Night, the spokesman of Diana, assails the maiden Flora for forsaking her virginity. But Zepherus reminds her that

> *Nature ordained not Men to liue alone,*
> *Where there are two a Woman should be one.*

Then Hesperus comes to appease Night's wrath, allowing her to transform the golden trees, metamorphosed by
the angry Diana, into their true shapes as knights of
Phoebus.

> *And now blithe Night*
> *Begins to shake off melancholy quite.*

and decides to have the trees dance (anti-masque):

> *. . . Ioy, trees! the time drawes neere*
> *When in your better formes you shall appeare.*
> *Dauncing and musicke must prepare the way,*
> *Ther's little tedious time in such delay.*

This spoken, the foure *Siluans* played on their instruments the
first straine of this song following: & at the repetition thereof
the voices fell in with the instruments which were thus de-
uided, a treble and a base were placed neere his Maiestie, and
an other treble and base neere the groue, that the words of
the song might be heard of all, because the trees of gould
instantly at the first sound of their voices began to moue,
and dance according to the measure of the time which the
musitians kept in singing, and the nature of the wordes which
they deliuered.

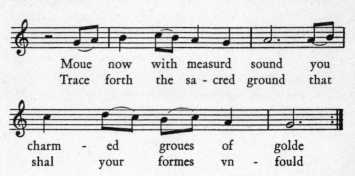

Moue   now   with measurd   sound   you
Trace   forth   the sa - cred   ground   that

charm - ed   groues   of   golde
shal   your   formes   vn - fould

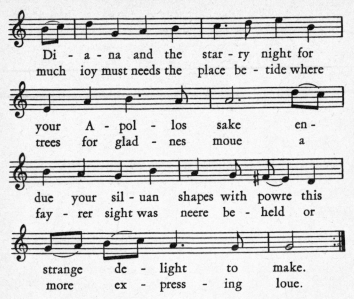

Di - a - na and the star - ry night for
much ioy must needs the place be - tide where

your A - pol - los sake en -
trees for glad - nes moue a

due your sil - uan shapes with powre this
fay - rer sight was neere be - held or

strange de - light to make.
more ex - press - ing loue.

Thus the transformation continues while the music hides the noise of the stage machinery. When the nine maskers stand in place of the trees, the music changes to a chorus.

This *Chorus* was in manner of an Eccho, seconded by the Cornets, then by the consort of ten, then by the consort of twelue, and by a double *Chorus* of voices standing on either side,— which kinde of harmony so distinguisht by the place, and by the seuerall nature of instruments, and changeable conueyance of the song, and performed by so many excellent masters, as were actors in that musicke, (their number in all amounting to fortie two voyces and instruments) could not but yeeld great satisfaction to the hearers.

After some elaborate dancing, a procession begins and . . . all this time of procession the six Cornets and six Chappell voices sung a sollemne motet . . . The motet beeing ended the Violins began the third new dance, which was liuely performed by the Maskers, after which they tooke forth the Ladies, and danc't the measures with them, which being finisht, the Maskers brought the Ladies back againe to their places;

Note that the traditional dancing finale was now in full swing, and that the audience joined in as was the custom. After this farewells were made and much music followed with songs, choruses, and dances. A final chorus was then performed 'with seuerall Ecchoes of musicke, and voices . . . At the end whereof the Maskers, putting off their visards, & helmets, made a low honour to the King, and attended his Ma: to the banquetting place.'

Thus did music dominate Campion's conception of the masque. At the same time, the whole show was a great burst of poetic imagination and brilliant pageantry. The story was a slim affair, but that, in Campion's estimation, did not matter so long as his audience was pleased. Beauty of lyric song, instrumental and vocal effects could carry the evening. The masques were short, light affairs. Was dramatic interest necessary? Campion thought not.

The sustained lyric quality that will be found in the songs and the masques themselves is a tribute to Campion's genius. Two of his best songs were included in the above sketch with their music. Generally these songs were closely related to the matter of the masque. A fine example of this was illustrated in 'Aduance your chorall

motions now' in the *Lords Maske*. Still another lyric in
this same work is worthy of quotation.

> *Wooe her, and win her, he that can:*
>   *Each woman hath two louers,*
> *So shee must take and leaue a man,*
>   *Till time more grace discouers.*
> *This doth* Loue *to shew that want*
>   *Makes beautie most respected;*
> *If faire women were more skant,*
>   *They would be more affected.*
>
> *Courtship and Musicke suite with loue,*
>   *They both are workes of passion;*
> *Happie is he whose works can moue*
>   *Yet sweete notes helpe perswasion.*
> *Mixe your words with Musicke then,*
>   *That they the more may enter;*
> *Bold assaults are fit for men,*
>   *That on strange beauties venture.*

The concluding songs of both the 1613 masques reveal
the practical, straight-forward Campion sensing the situation at the close of the entertainment and giving it a
dash of freshness by a short lively song, as, for instance,
at the end of the *Lords Maske*;

> *No longer wrong the night*
> *Of her* Hymenoean *right;*
> *A thousand* Cupids *call away,*
> *Fearing the approaching day;*
> *The Cocks alreadie crow:*
>   *Dance then and goe.*

This practical side of Campion that these final songs suggest has not been stressed. The foregoing development of the various aspects of his writing must, however, have created such an impression. In fact, this practicality that is so strongly brought out in his masque writing is one of Campion's admirable traits. Fundamentally sound, it served him well in almost every case. It might even be considered at the root of his success especially as a poet-musician. But does it not also lie at the bottom of the simplicity and directness of his music and his theories on music? Is it not an intrinsic part of his conception of the masque as entertainment? Is it not reflected in the diligent care with which the music and musicians are handled in them? The answer would seem to be in the affirmative.

Then with his lyric and musical powers united to this practical-mindedness, Campion should stand out as a successful poet-musician. He was so recognized in his own time. There seems to be little cause now to doubt the justice of this reputation.

IX

CONCLUSION

THE foregoing study has had as its purpose the consideration of the interrelations of poetry and music in Elizabethan days, and a discussion of the causes of the gradual separation of the two arts in the seventeenth and eighteenth centuries. It has attempted to explain more fully than has hitherto been possible some of the reasons for the clearness, the freshness, and the spontaneity of Elizabethan lyrical poetry with special reference to the work of Thomas Campion in which these qualities are most happily joined.

From the facts presented, it is now clear how it took centuries of folk-song to produce the Elizabethan lyric, and how the predominance of music during the Elizabethan period, which is acknowledged as the time of England's greatest creative activity, had a material effect on the formation of the poetry. The reason for this influence was that in this age both music and poetry were vocal, that poets wrote lyrics to be sung and composers sought singable lyrics. This vocal music was different from our general conception of music, which most people believe began about three centuries ago, because it was, for the most part, inseparably associated with words, even dependent on words for rhythm and melody. Because the rhythm of Elizabethan music was free from all fetters, bar lines, and time signatures, the words took on the

cadenced flow of natural music, each word joining the
next not according to some prescribed measure, but as the
meaning and the sense dictated. The result, of course,
was irregularity of phrasing and a variety of verse forms.
The melody arose out of the natural inflections of the
spoken poetry. At the same time, the words were dependent on the music for the expression of emotion; the
thought was simple, and because of this simplicity the
words were concrete. Therefore, according to the musical
practice of the period, the lyric style was plain in order
to allow the perfect adaptation of musical rhythms, the
freedom of which brought a flowing stream of pure
sound; a melody which sprang up spontaneously from
the inherent music in the utterance of the spoken words;
a mood which conveyed, through musical sound, the full
expression of the intense feeling which was the inspiration of their creation.

Thus the musical style not only conditioned the words
of a single stanza designed for a musical setting, but also
conditioned the form and content of lyrics written in
several stanzas, some of which were combined into the
sonnet form. Repeated practice along these lines naturally
led to the establishment of what is now recognized as
the typical form of the Elizabethan lyric. Our study of
Campion has called attention to the perfect union of music and verse that he achieved under these conditions,
and, as a result, suggests a general re-estimation of
Elizabethan and English lyrical poetry.

Since the bulk of English vocal music before 1600 was
concerted, that is to say written for many voices, it is
now clear how Campion in 1601 shifted the balance from

the part-song to the solo-song in authorizing the publication of *A Booke of Ayres*, the significance of which has been generally overlooked. This change of emphasis brought the words of Elizabethan song into such prominence that they became equally important with the music since the word-phrases of these ayres are the exact counterparts of the simple and tuneful melodies. In a period when poets deliberately provided lyrics for music, and composers demanded a certain type of lyric for this purpose, Campion, of course, represents the ideal, because he had the talent for both poetry and music. It has therefore been shown how necessary it is to add the role of musician to a consideration of Campion as a poet. But since Campion himself declared that music guided his creative impulse, that is to say, that he was as much a musician as a poet, he must henceforth be considered in reality as a musical poet.

In common with his contemporaries, Campion made free use of the analogies of poetry and music current at the time. The chief points in his treatise on poetry hinge on the understanding of these analogies for he learned from music the true nature of quantity in English poetry. In fact Campion unconsciously advocated a musical prosody in the writing of his ayres by marking the scansion quantitatively with musical notation. Again, in turning his attention to the smoothness of verse without the additional ornament of rime, he showed that the cadence of verse lies not in its rime but in its rhythm. He was led by his musician's ear into this virgin territory and formed his music and verse so that the one is generally incomplete without the other. In fact, the one explains the

other not only in the matter of repeated word-phrases
for effective or epigrammatic meanings which can only
be appreciated by studying the *ayres*; but also in the irregularities of verse phrasing, and the musical inflections
of the speech melody. So apt are his musical counterparts of the words that the relationship of music and
verse found in his ayres is unapproached. Furthermore,
in writing his masques Campion worked from the practical point of view of creating musical entertainments,
and the *Lord Hayes Maske* is the unique testimony of the
work of a musical poet.

Campion's ayres, however, remain the everlasting record of the interrelation of the two arts in this Elizabethan period. From the creative point of view, Campion
was compelled to express himself as he did because in the
impulse that brought the words and notes into the mind
of the composer simultaneously rests the freshness and
spontaneity of the ayres, while sheer simplicity of expression inspired a flow of beautiful verbal and musical
melody touched with the emotion of genuine feeling.
Ayres have their art, and the practice of that art, as
Campion said, 'will be much for him to doe that hath
no power over both [words and notes].' Since this union
is the *summum bonum* of an ideal lyric poet, and since his
ayres attain such a high quality, Campion must be reckoned among those few chosen lyric poets who have
approached nearest to the old ideal.

BIBLIOGRAPHY

The following comprehensive list of books is specially selected *as related to the general subject matter of this study.*

Ambros,A.W., *The Boundaries of Music and Poetry*, New York, 1893.

Beers,H.A., *Points at Issue*, New York, London, 1904. Cf. 'The English Lyric.'

Brooke,T., *The Shakespeare Songs*, New York, 1929.

Brown,J., *A Dissertation on the Rise, Union and Power . . . of Poetry and Music*, London, 1763.

Bullen,A.H., *Lyrics from the Song-Books of the Elizabethan Age*, London, 1886.

Bullen,A.H., *More Lyrics from the Song-Books of the Elizabethan Age*, London, 1888.

Bullen,A.H., *Works of Thomas Campion*, London, 1889.

Bullen,A.H., *Thomas Campion, Songs and Masques*, London and New York, 1903. A brief comment on Campion's music by Janet Dodge is included in the introduction.

Bullen,A.H., *Elizabethans*, London, 1924.

Burney, Dr.C., *A General History of Music*, London, 1776–89.

The Cambridge History of English Literature, Edited by A.W.Ward and A.R.Waller, New York and Cambridge, 1909, VOL.IV, Chapter VI, 'The Song-Books and Miscellanies,' p.127; Chapter VIII, 'Thomas Campion,' p.163.

Chappell,W., *Popular Music of the Olden Time*, London, 1855; Revised 1893.

Cowling,G.H., *Music on the Shakesperian Stage*, Cambridge, 1913.

Cox,F.A., *English Madrigals in the Time of Shakespeare*, London, [1899].

Davey,H., *History of English Music*, London, [1895], 1921.

Deakin,A., *Outlines of Musical Bibliography*, Birmingham, 1899.

Dent,E.J., *Foundations of English Opera*, Cambridge, 1928.

Elson,L.C., *Shakespeare in Music*, Boston, 1901.

Evans,W.M., *Ben Jonson and Elizabethan Music*, Lancaster, 1929.

Fellowes,E.H., *English Madrigal Verse*, Oxford, 1920.

Fellowes,E.H., *The English Madrigal School*, in 36 volumes, London, 1913–24.

Fellowes,E.H., *The English School of Lutenist Song Writers*, London, 1920–25.

'Second Series' with Thomas Campion's Ayres, 1926.

Fellowes,E.H., *English Madrigal Composers*, Oxford, 1921.

Fellowes,E.H., *The English Madrigal*, London, 1925.

Fox-Strangways,A.H., *Essays and Studies of the English Association*, Oxford, 1921. 'Words and Music in Song.'

Gibbon,J.M., *Melody and the Lyric*, London and Toronto, 1930.

Glyn,M.H., *About Elizabethan Virginal Music and Its Composers*, London, [1924].

Hadow,W.H., *Collected Essays*, London, 1928. Cf. 'William Byrd,' p.41; 'A Comparison of Poetry and Music,' p.220.

Hawkins, Sir J., *General History of the Science and Practice of Music*, London, 1776.

Herford,C.H., and Simpson,P., *Ben Jonson*, Oxford, 1925–27. Cf.VOL.II, 'Masques and Entertainments,' p.247.

Lanier,S., *The Science of English Verse*, New York, 1880.

Lanier,S., *Music and Poetry*, New York, 1898.

Lindsey,E.S., *The Music in Ben Jonson's Plays. Modern Language Notes*, XLIV, p.86.

Lindsey,E.S., *The Music of the Songs in Fletcher's Plays, Studies in Philology*, VOL.XXI, p.325, VOL.XXVI, p.425.

MacDonagh,T., *Thomas Campion and the Art of English Poetry*, Dublin, 1913.

Mason,D.G., *The Art of Music*, New York, 1915, VOLS.I AND V.

Mason,J., *An Essay on the Power of Numbers, and the Principles of Harmony in Poetical Compositions*, London, 1749.

More,P.E., *Shelburne Essays*, First Series, New York and London, 1904. 'The Science of English Verse.'

Morris,R.O., *Contrapuntal Technique in the Sixteenth Century*, Oxford, 1922.

Nagel,W., *Geschichte der Musik in England*, Strassburg, 1894.

Naylor,E.W., *Shakespeare and Music*, London, 1896.

Noble,R., *Shakespeare's Use of Song*, London, 1923.

Omond,T.S., *English Metrists*, Oxford, 1921.

Omond,T.S., *A Study of Metre*, London, [1903], 1920.

Palgrave,F.T., *Golden Treasure of Songs and Lyrics*, [1861], Fowler edition, London, 1921, 1924.

Periodicals such as the *Musical Antiquary*, London and New York, 1909–13; *The Musical Quarterly*, New York, 1915–; *Music and Letters*, London, 1920–, for a variety of subjects.

Pratt,W.S., *The New Encyclopedia of Music and Musicians*, New York, [1924], 1929.

Reed,E.B., *English Lyrical Poetry*, New Haven, 1912, which supersedes J.Erskine's *The Elizabethan Lyric*, New York, 1903.

Schelling,F.E., *The Queens Progress and Other Elizabethan Sketches*, Boston and New York, 1904, p.71ff.

Shakespeare's England, Oxford, 1916, VOL.II, 'Music,' by W.Barclay Squire, p.15.

Sherman,S.P., *Shaping Men and Women*, Garden City, 1928, 'Thomas Campion,' p.158.

Smith,G.G., *Elizabethan Critical Essays*, Oxford, 1904.

Spingarn,J.E., *A History of Literary Criticism in the Renaissance*, New York, 1925.

Thompson,G.A., *Elizabethan Criticism of Poetry*, Menasha, 1924.

Vivian,P., *Campion's Works*, Oxford, 1909.

Walker,E., *A History of Music in England*, London, [1907] 1924.

Warlock,P., *The English Ayre*, London, 1926.

Webb,D., *Observations on the Correspondence between Poetry and Music*, London, 1769.

Wilson,K.M., *The Real Rhythm in English Poetry*, Aberdeen, 1929.

Wilson,K.M., *Sound and Meaning in English Poetry*, London and Toronto, 1930.